Joseph Butler

FIVE SERMONS

PREACHED AT THE ROLLS CHAPEL

and

A DISSERTATION UPON THE

NATURE OF VIRTUE

Edited, with introduction and notes,
by STEPHEN L. DARWALL

HACKETT PUBLISHING COMPANY

JOSEPH BUTLER: 1692–1752

Cover design by Richard L. Listenberger
Interior design by James N. Rogers

For further information, please address
    Hackett Publishing Company
    P.O. Box 44937
    Indianapolis, Indiana 46204

95 94 93 92 91 90   3 4 5 6 7 8 9 10

Library of Congress Cataloging in Publication Data

Butler, Joseph, 1692–1752
    Five sermons, preached at the Rolls Chapel and A
dissertation upon the nature of virtue.

    Bibliography: p.
    Includes index.
    1. Church of England—Sermons.   2. Anglican Communion—
Sermons. 3. Sermons, English. 4. Ethics. I. Darwall,
Stephen L., 1946–   .   II. Title.
BX5133.B87F55   1983   252'.03   83–12577
ISBN 0–915145–61–8 (pbk.)

TABLE OF CONTENTS

INTRODUCTION

When David Hume listed "Dr. Butler" in the Introduction to his *Treatise of Human Nature* as one of "some late philosophers in England, who have begun to put the science of man on a new footing," he was judging Butler on the strength of a few sermons preached at the Rolls Chapel and published as part of a collection in 1726. This fact displays the central paradox of Joseph Butler's life and work. On the one hand, he was an Anglican clergyman who devoted his life mainly to church affairs and whose major work, *An Analogy of Religion,* was a lengthy defense of Christian orthodoxy against deistic natural theology, a work now largely of historical interest. On the other, Butler was an acute philosophical thinker who, in a few short essays, mostly sermons, sketched a view of ethics and moral psychology which, while incomplete in details, has influenced moral philosophy ever since. Although it was Butler the churchman and author of the *Analogy* who was best known during his lifetime, it has been Butler the moral philosopher and author—primarily of the works collected in this short volume—who has had an enduring impact.[1]

"There are two ways," Butler wrote in the Preface to the *Sermons,* "in which the subject of morals may be treated. One begins from inquiring into the abstract relations of things; the other from a matter of fact, namely, what the particular nature of man is. . . ." (p. 13) Significantly, Butler's choice of method was the latter. Unlike his rationalist predecessor Samuel Clarke, Butler aimed in the *Sermons* to relate ethics to an empirically adequate understanding of human nature—to what Hume called "the science of man."

When Butler wrote the *Sermons,* there was a pressing need for such a treatment of ethics. Thomas Hobbes had argued forcefully in the *Leviathan,* published in 1651, that a scientific account of human nature leaves no place for ethics as traditionally conceived. Hobbes held that human conduct results from whatever desire or aversion is strongest in a person at any given time. He argued that the traditional hypothesis of a special faculty, through which we can know what we ought to do and determine our conduct accordingly, is empirically baseless. Moreover, the only content that can be given to a traditional moralist's two favorite notions, the good and the right, comes, respectively, from our own actual desires and from the orders of a political sovereign who is sufficiently powerful to compel obedience. What any man calls good, Hobbes wrote, is simply "whatsoever is the object of . . . [his] appetite or desire." There is no "common rule of good and evil, to be taken from the nature of the objects

---

1. The present volume includes five of the *Fifteen Sermons Preached at the Rolls Chapel* along with "A Dissertation upon the Nature of Virtue." Almost every influential idea and argument of Butler's can be found in these selections. Reference to the *Sermons* is to page numbers of the present volume.

1

themselves."[2] Nor is any conduct in itself either just or unjust: "Where there is no common power, there is no law: where no law, no injustice."[3] Justice can be measured only by the actual legislation of political authority and not by any independent critical standard. So Hobbes had thrown down the gauntlet: a scientific understanding of man reveals no "ethical" faculty in human nature, and demonstrates both that the good is subjective and that the right is conventional.

As if this were not enough, Hobbes went on to argue, along with other writers such as Mandeville, that an empirical approach to man shows also that human desires are at their base more self-regarding than traditional moralists had been wont to suppose. He maintained that even such seemingly other-regarding motives as charity and parental affection are thinly disguised desires for personal power.

Butler's choice of method, then, was at least partly a response to the Hobbesian challenge. It was an attempt to show, as against Hobbes, that a careful study of human nature reveals something far more complicated, subtle, and interesting than Hobbes had found. More important for a moralist's purposes, Butler maintained that it reveals what he called the "moral institution of life." To be a fully human agent, Butler argued, is to apprehend oneself and one's life through irreducibly ethical categories.

If the *Sermons* demonstrated that an empirically adequate understanding of man is incomplete without the ethical dimension, it did not settle for Butler's successors the precise contours of our ethical nature. In particular, it left open what was to become the major question of eighteenth-century moral philosophy: whether ethics is primarily a matter of reason or of sentiment. Butler was not completely clear on this point himself. His candidate for the human ethical faculty, conscience—or, as he also called it, "the principle of reflection"—appears to have elements of both reason and sentiment. In the *Dissertation* he refers to its deliverance as a "sentiment of the understanding" or a "perception of the heart," terms that seem to straddle what later eighteenth-century writers would argue to be an unbridgeable gulf. In this connection, it is significant that different elements of Butler's view anticipate the two main opposing positions on this central issue of eighteenth-century (and contemporary) moral philosophy: those of Immanuel Kant and David Hume.

Hume's notion of a moral sense or sentiment, for example, is a direct descendant of Butler's principle of reflection or conscience. While there is ample evidence that Butler did not think of the principle of reflection as involving sentiment *as opposed to* reason, he described it, at least occasionally, as involving, like Hume's moral sense, a reflective sentiment *felt* from a dispassionate and disinterested point of view. For example, in presenting evidence in Sermon I for the existence of human conscience

2. Thomas Hobbes, *Leviathan,* ed. Michael Oakeshott (Oxford, Basil Blackwell, 1955), p. 32.

3. *Ibid.,* p. 83.

(p. 30), Butler asks us to imagine a man considering two different acts he has committed, one of charity and the other of cruelty: "let the man . . . coolly reflect upon them afterwards, without regard to their consequences to himself: to assert that any common man would be affected in the same way towards these different actions . . . , but approve or disapprove them equally, is too glaring a falsity to need being confuted." Here, Butler appears to maintain that conscience is our capacity to view our acts and motives from a certain reflective perspective and to have sentiments or affections towards them.

But if Hume's moral sentimentalism derives from Butler, it is also clear that other elements of Butler's view anticipate themes often cited as Kant's unique contribution to ethics. Butler held that moral demands could not consist of rules or laws that are simply imposed on us, "from the outside," as it were. Moral agency requires a capacity to make *our own judgments* regarding the moral character of our acts and motives. It requires a faculty, the principle of reflection, that makes us, as he says, a "law to ourselves." (p. 37). The principle of reflection, then, plays the same role for Butler that practical reason would later play for Kant. It is a faculty that is necessary for moral agency and whose existence makes a person a "law to himself." Butler's very phrasing of this latter point suggests Kant's idea that moral laws are in an important sense self-legislated.

Probably no figure had a greater impact on nineteenth-century British moral philosophy than Butler.[4] The *Sermons* were reprinted more frequently during that period than any other ethical work, and both the utilitarians and their critics borrowed extensively from his ideas. Butler's influence on Henry Sidgwick was especially profound; his *Methods of Ethics* is full of references to the *Sermons*. Of particular interest is the way Sidgwick utilized Butler's theme in Sermon XI (IV in the present volume): that we can often best achieve an end by *not* constantly and directly trying to achieve it. Butler was primarily concerned with the way in which people often defeat their own purpose if they concentrate strictly on promoting their own happiness (Sidgwick called this the "paradox of egoistic hedonism"). The general point has even wider application, however, as Butler realized. In particular, it allowed a utilitarian moralist such as Sidgwick, who took universal happiness to be the fundamental ethical end, to deny that "Universal Benevolence is . . . always (the) best motive of action."[5]

The development of ethical intuitionism in the early twentieth century also owed a debt to Butler. Significantly, a quote from the *Sermons* served as the epigraph for G. E. Moore's seminal work of twentieth-century Brit-

---

4. Jerome B. Schneewind, *Sidgwick's Ethics and Victorian Moral Philosophy* (Oxford: Oxford University Press, 1977), p. 7. This book has an excellent account of Butler's importance for nineteenth-century English ethics, particularly his influence on Sidgwick.

5. Henry Sidgwick, *The Methods of Ethics* (Indpls.: Hackett, 1981) , p. 413.

ish intuitionism, *Principia Ethica.* Butler had admonished his contemporaries not to confuse distinct motives or "principles": "Everything is what it is and not another thing." Moore similarly complained that his contemporaries often confused such ethical properties as goodness with other "natural" properties such as "being desired" and "pleasant," or with other metaphysical properties such as "being commanded by God."

What Moore derived from Butler was not simply a taste for precise philosophical distinctions. In Sermon II, Butler had argued that the principle of reflection involves in its very conception "judgment, direction, superintendency" (p. 39). That is, to form an adequate idea of conscience, we must already make "the distinction, which everybody is acquainted with, between *mere power* and *authority*" (p. 39). For Butler, the problem with Hobbes's theory of human nature was that it left out of account our capacity for determining our conduct by ethical and value *judgments;* that is, by a faculty that we implicitly regard as morally authoritative independently of its strength as a motive. Butler's point was that the *authority* of conscience, an ethical notion, is irreducible to any fact, regarding how it *actually* functions as a motive; for example, its psychological strength. Moore's attack on what he called naturalism in ethics, then, is a successor to Butler's response to Hobbes.

It is worth considering Butler's response to the Hobbesian challenge in more detail. What gave Hobbes's challenge its point was the demand for evidence and certainty that characterized the rise of modern philosophy and science in the seventeenth century. While earlier writers might accept the proposition that certain ethical principles are simply self-evident to reason or received through revelation, this no longer seemed to be a viable position if, as Hobbes proposed, a scientific account of man could be given without any reference either to ethical principles or to a faculty for apprehending them.

For Hobbes, a human being is best thought of as a kind of mechanical system whose movement results from forces operating on him. Even self-generated movement, Hobbes believed, results from internal forces. We call "desire," Hobbes wrote, those forces or "endeavours," those "small beginnings of motion, within the body of man, before they appear in walking, speaking, striking, and other visible action."[6]

Butler agreed with Hobbes that our psychology must be viewed as a kind of natural system. What he denied was that human beings are *mechanical* systems. If human conduct were simply the result of whatever desire happened to be strongest, we would not be genuine *agents;* our acts and lives would not be in our own hands. Human beings are not simply collections of desires and aversions, of internal forces whose vector sum determines what they do. Rather, they act. Through the capacity to reflect, especially from points of view that are more or less dispassionate and disinterested, *and* through the capacity to have *considered* desires and aversions from those points of view, they are capable of expressing in conduct

6. Hobbes, *Leviathan,* p. 31.

their own considered judgments of what it is best, appropriate, and fitting, to do. Because man has a principle of reflection, he can act as a unified agent. "A machine," Butler wrote, "is inanimate and passive, but we are agents. Our constitution is put in our own power" (p. 15).

This view connects closely with Butler's theme that "virtue consists in following, and vice in deviating from" the nature of man. The nature of other animals may, perhaps, consist in simply acting on the strongest desire of the moment, but this is not so with human beings. Our distinctive nature includes a capacity for agency, for self-directed action. But this, Butler argues, involves acting in conformity to an authoritative principle, the principle of reflection, of conscience. So virtue is consonant with human nature and vice disconsonant.

Butler was simply recalling a theme of Plato's: the self is an ordered hierarchical whole whose different parts can come into conflict, threatening disorder, and indeed, dissolution of the self. There is within the self, however, a principle whose office is to settle conflict between lower principles and maintain order through its *judgments* of what is best. For Plato, the ordering principle is *nous,* or reason, which enables us to know what is really valuable, namely, the Form of the Good. Butler adapts Plato's ordering principle without committing himself to Plato's metaphysics. It is enough, Butler seems to say, that we can all adopt a dispassionate and disinterested standpoint from which to assess our acts and motives, and that when we do so, we can find agreement in our judgments. Thus Butler combines Plato's insight that the unity of the self depends on an evaluative order achieved through a faculty of practical judgment with a nonmetaphysical, naturalistic account of the required faculty. This version makes Plato's view more palatable to the modern age.

One of the most enduring of Butler's contributions to the history of ethics has been his critique of psychological theories that seek to reduce all motivation to some dominant self-regarding desire, such as the general desire for one's own pleasure or happiness in life. Butler's arguments were directed primarily at Hobbes and such contemporaries as Bernard Mandeville, whose *Fable of the Bees* had been published in 1714, but they are equally relevant to reductionist psychological theories today.

Butler's general conceptual argument has often been regarded as a conclusive refutation of the view that we desire only our own happiness for its own sake, and anything else only for the sake of it. Pleasure or happiness itself, he writes, "consists only in the enjoyment of those objects which are by nature suited to our several particular appetites, passions, and affections" (p. 48). Whenever a person derives pleasure or happiness, there must be something *from which* pleasure or happiness is derived; there must be an *object* of the person's pleasure or happiness. Moreover, for something to be an object of pleasure or happiness, it must be something that we can like, enjoy, or desire for itself, for its own sake. Thus, if a person derives pleasure from "eating food more than from swallowing a stone" (p. 47), this is because the former, though not the latter, is something that he likes or enjoys for itself. Butler is sometimes interpreted as being committed here to the position that the pleasure resulting from something occurs only if there was a prior *desire* for that thing, thus ruling out spontaneous, undesired pleasures, such as the pleasure of an unexpected viewing of a spectacular sunset. But this need not be the case. All Butler needs to assert is that, for pleasure and happiness to occur, there must be an underlying disposition to respond favorably and directly to that in which pleasure is taken; for example, looking at the sunset.

Even so, Butler may be overstating his conclusion; for he says "that all particular appetites and passions are toward *external things themselves*" (p. 47). A sophisticated defender of the position that all desires are self-regarding might attempt to evade Butler's argument in the following way: Even if a person's desires have different objects, and are not simply for one's own *pleasure* as such, they are never for "external things themselves"; rather, they always aim at different experiences or states of mind *of the desirer* that he or she finds intrinsically pleasurable. This thesis is immune to Butler's general argument against confusing self-love with other desires and is also an interesting position in its own right.

Butler's second line of attack against this more sophisticated position is to note first that the point at issue is an empirical one. Once this is granted, he thinks we can find a great deal of evidence showing that people have many desires that are essentially *other-involving* and that have as their objects that certain states of affairs involving others *actually obtain*. Accordingly, these desires cannot simply be directed to certain psychological states of the experiencer. Throughout Sermon I, Butler provides an impressive list of such desires: desire of esteem from others, indignation against successful vice, desire for revenge, fear of disgrace, covetousness, love, and hate, among many others. Each involves a desire for a state of affairs, essentially including another person. The desire for esteem, for instance, is the desire for others actually to esteem us, and is not simply for the experience of *thinking* that they do, although we may desire to *know* that they do *also*.

In a lengthy footnote to the first Sermon aimed at Hobbes, Butler marshals evidence that human beings also have *other-regarding,* or benevolent, desires and not simply other-involving ones (pp. 26–28n). For example, it is quite normal for people to be pleased by the simple knowledge that a friend is flourishing. When we put this evidence together, Butler believes that we have as strong a case for the existence of benevolent desires as there could be, "supposing there was this affection in our nature." That is, we could only have stronger evidence for the existence of other-regarding and other social desires if it were not, as it is, a "mere question of fact or natural history."

Having established that we do in fact have benevolent and other social desires, Butler proceeds in Sermon IV to argue that there is no incompatibility between benevolence and self-love; indeed, the two motives largely complement each other. His aim is to convince anyone who believes it is rational to promote *one's own* interest that it is also rational, on that person's own view, to act *for the sake of* others; that is, to be motivated by benevolence.

Butler makes the important point that, even if our primary concern were to have the happiest life possible, it would by no means follow that we should always, or even normally, concentrate on our own interests, in deciding what to do. Sidgwick referred to this as the "paradox of egoism," but the general point is not restricted to the end of personal happiness. Deciding what to do, act by act, by *considering* which act is most likely to promote a given end, may not actually promote that end. Sometimes deliberately *trying* to promote an end may actually frustrate its promotion. Butler argues that this general possibility is especially true if the end is one's own happiness, since *that* end can only be realized through the satisfaction of *other* desires. Furthermore, "disengagement is absolutely necessary to enjoyment; and a person may have so steady an eye upon his own interest . . . as may hinder him *attending* to many gratifications within his reach" (pp. 49-50). Add to this the fact that, for most people, an important part of happiness includes personal relationships and human fellowship—that "the greatest satisfactions to ourselves depend upon our having benevolence in a due degree" (p. 27)—and we are led to his conclusion that "how much soever a paradox it may appear, it is certainly true that even from self-love we should endeavor to get over all inordinate regard to and consideration of ourselves," (p. 49) and to cultivate other-regarding desires.

The general point involved in the paradox of egoism can also arise with respect to other ends. In particular, it can appear in connection with the end that is the object of general benevolence, the greatest happiness of all. Butler notes that our considered judgments of conscience do not approve of all and only disinterestedly benevolent behavior: "we are constituted so as to condemn falsehood, unprovoked violence, injustice, and to approve of benevolence to some, preferably to others, abstracted from all consideration which conduct is likeliest to produce an overbalance of happiness or misery" (p. 73). Such examples anticipate much of what would become a standard litany of objections to utilitarianism when it was formulated in the nineteenth century. General utility cannot provide a standard of right conduct, objected the critics, for we manifestly disapprove of acts of lying, assault, and injustice in themselves and not because of their relation to utility. Moreover, they argued, we often approve of giving partial concern to family and friends even though a utilitarian would presumably think, like Bentham, that "each [person] is to count for one and no more than one."

Butler not only provided the critics of utilitarianism with some of their most persuasive counterexamples, but also showed the utilitarians their most promising line of defense. Although *we* have dispositions to disapprove and approve of acts and motives independently of our perceiving their utility, Butler suggests that this is quite consistent with "the good of creation be(ing) the only end of the Author of it" (p. 66). Here we see another version of the general point involved in the paradox of egoism, that is, one we might call the paradox of universal benevolence. General happiness may best be promoted if men act out of motives other than general benevolence. In particular, a person may best promote general happiness, the utilitarian can argue, if he or she gives independent weight in actual decision-making to such matters as truthfulness, justice, family obligations, and so on. This position may be held by either act or rule utilitarians; that is, either by those who take the utility directly promoted by a specific act as the criterion of its rightness, or those who take the utility of people generally following a rule under which an act fits, as a criterion of the act's rightness. The latter is easiest to see. Many utilitarians following Mill have argued that we should give weight to such matters as rights and justice since our *generally* so doing maximizes utility. But the former is also a respectable position and many utilitarians, such as Sidgwick, have held it. Butler's influence on Sidgwick is evident here when the latter writes, "The doctrine that Universal Happiness is the ultimate *standard* must not be understood to imply that Universal Benevolence is . . . always (the) best *motive* of action." For a number of reasons we may be more likely to perform acts that *actually* maximize universal happiness if we can, when appropriate, avert our eye from that goal and act from other motives.[7]

The controversy between utilitarianism and its critics continues vigorously on these points today. In this instance, as in many other current debates in moral philosophy and philosophy of mind, Butler's thought has proven its enduring value.

A NOTE ON THE TEXT: The *Five Sermons* are, respectively, Sermons I, II, III, XI, and XII of *The Fifteen Sermons Preached at the Rolls Chapel.* The *Dissertation upon the Nature of Virtue* was originally appended to the first edition of the *Analogy of Religion* as "Dissertation II." These texts are given here in their entirety, as is Butler's Preface to the *Sermons,* except for a few paragraphs that refer to sermons not included in this edition.

---

7. In thinking about the issues discussed in this Introduction, I have benefited from discussions with Nicholas Sturgeon and Peter Railton, and, over the years, with David Falk. I am also indebted to John Lachs and Sheldon Peterfreund who provided helpful comments on earlier drafts.

SELECTED BIBLIOGRAPHY

Butler's Works

The authoritative edition of Butler's collected works is *The Works of Joseph Butler*, Introduction and Notes by J. H. Bernard. (London: The English Theological Library, 1900), 2 vols. In addition to *Fifteen Sermons Preached at the Rolls Chapel,* it includes *The Analogy of Religion, Six Sermons Preached Upon Public Occasions,* the essays on virtue and personal identity, and some other materials.

Books on Butler's Ethics

C. D. Broad. *Five Types of Ethical Theory,* ch. 3. (Paterson, N. J.: Littlefield, Adams & Co., 1959).

Austin E. Duncan-Jones. *Butler's Moral Philosophy.* (Harmondsworth: Penguin Books, 1952).

Ernest C. Mossner. *Bishop Butler and the Age of Reason.* (New York: Macmillan, 1936).

Thomas Aerwyn Roberts. *The Concept of Benevolence: Aspects of Eighteenth Century Moral Philosophy.* (London: Macmillan, 1973).

Articles on Butler's Ethics

Reginald Jackson. "Bishop Butler's Refutation of Psychological Hedonism," *Philosophy* 18 (1943), 114–139.

John Kleinig. "Butler in a Cool Hour," *Journal of the History of Philosophy* 7 (1969), 399–411.

Edmund Leites. "A Problem in Joseph Butler's Ethics," *Southwestern Journal of Philosophy* 6 (1975), 43–57.

Thomas H. McPherson. "The Development of Bishop Butler's Ethics, I and II," *Philosophy* 23 (1948), 317–331, 24 (1949), 3–22.

Michael S. Pritchard. "Conscience and Reason in Butler's Ethics," *Southwestern Journal of Philosophy* 9 (1978), 39–49.

D. Daiches Raphael. "Bishop Butler's View of Conscience," *Philosophy* 24 (1949), 219–238.

Amélie O. Rorty. "Butler on Benevolence and Conscience," *Philosophy* 53 (1978), 171–184.

Nicholas L. Sturgeon. "Nature and Conscience in Butler's Ethics," *Philosophical Review* 85 (1976), 316–356.

A. E. Taylor. "Some Features of Butler's Ethics," *Mind* 35 (1926), 273–300.

Alan R. White. "Conscience and Self-Love in Butler's Sermons," *Philosophy* 27 (1952), 329–344.

THE PREFACE

[1] THOUGH it is scarce possible to avoid judging, in some way or other, of almost everything which offers itself to one's thoughts, yet it is certain that many persons, from different causes, never exercise their judgment, upon what comes before them, in the way of determining whether it be conclusive and holds. They are perhaps entertained with some things, not so with others; they like, and they dislike; but whether that which is proposed to be made out be really made out or not, whether a matter be stated according to the real truth of the case, seems to the generality of people merely a circumstance of no consideration at all. Arguments are often wanted for some accidental purpose; but proof as such is what they never want for themselves, for their own satisfaction of mind or conduct in life. Not to mention the multitudes who read merely for the sake of talking or to qualify themselves for the world, or some such kind of reasons; there are—even of the few who read for their own entertainment and have a real curiosity to see what is said—several, which is prodigious, who have no sort of curiosity to see what is true: I say curiosity, because it is too obvious to be mentioned how much that religious and sacred attention which is due to truth and to the important question, What is the rule of life? is lost out of the world.

[2] For the sake of this whole class of readers, for they are of different capacities, different kinds, and get into this way from different occasions, I have often wished that it had been the custom to lay before people nothing in matters of argument but premises and leave them to draw conclusions themselves; which, though it could not be done in all cases, might in many.

[3] The great number of books and papers of amusement, which, of one kind or another, daily come into one's way, have in part occasioned, and most perfectly fall in with and humor, this idle way of reading and considering things. By this means, time even in solitude is happily got rid of, without the pain of attention; neither is any part of it more put to the account of idleness, one can scarce forbear saying, is spent with less thought, than great part of that which is spent in reading.

[4] Thus people habituate themselves to let things pass through their minds, as one may speak, rather than to think of them. Thus by use they become satisfied merely with seeing what is said, without going any further. Review and attention, and even forming a judgment, becomes fatigue; and to lay anything before them that requires it, is putting them quite out of their way.

[5] There are also persons, and there are at least more of them than have a right to claim such superiority, who take for granted that they are acquainted with everything, and that no subject, if treated in the manner

11

it should be, can be treated in any manner but what is familiar and easy to them.

[6] It is true, indeed, that few persons have a right to demand attention; but it is also true that nothing can be understood without that degree of it which the very nature of the thing requires. Now morals, considered as a science, concerning which speculative difficulties are daily raised, and treated with regard to those difficulties, plainly require a very peculiar attention. For here ideas never are in themselves determinate, but become so by the train of reasoning and the place they stand in; since it is impossible that words can always stand for the same ideas, even in the same author, much less in different ones. Hence an argument may not readily be apprehended, which is different from its being mistaken; and even caution to avoid being mistaken may, in some cases, render it less readily apprehended. It is very unallowable for a work of imagination or entertainment not to be of easy comprehension, but may be unavoidable in a work of another kind where a man is not to form or accommodate, but to state things as he finds them.

[7] It must be acknowledged that some of the following discourses are very abstruse and difficult, or, if you please, obscure; but I must take leave to add that those alone are judges whether or no and how far this is a fault, who are judges whether or no and how far it might have been avoided—those only who will be at the trouble to understand what is here said and to see how far the things here insisted upon, and not other things, might have been put in a plainer manner; which yet I am very far from asserting that they could not.

[8] This much however will be allowed that general criticisms concerning obscurity considered as a distinct thing from confusion and perplexity of thought, as in some cases there may be ground for them; so in others, they may be nothing more at the bottom than complaints that everything is not to be understood with the same ease that some things are. Confusion and perplexity in writing is indeed without excuse, because anyone may, if he pleases, know whether he understands and sees through what he is about; and it is unpardonable for a man to lay his thoughts before others when he is conscious that he himself does not know whereabouts he is, or how the matter before him stands. It is coming abroad in disorder, which he ought to be dissatisfied to find himself in at home.

[9] But even obscurities arising from other causes than the abstruseness of the argument may not be always inexcusable. Thus a subject may be treated in a manner which all along supposes the reader acquainted with what has been said upon it, both by ancient and modern writers, and with what is the present state of opinion in the world concerning such subject. This will create a difficulty of a very peculiar kind, and even throw an obscurity over the whole before those who are not thus informed; but those who are will be disposed to excuse such a manner, and other things of the like kind, as a saving of their patience.

[10] However, upon the whole, as the title of sermons gives some right to expect what is plain and of easy comprehension, and as the best audi-

tories are mixed, I shall not set about to justify the propriety of preaching, or under that title publishing, discourses so abstruse as some of these are; neither is it worth while to trouble the reader with the account of my doing either. He must not however impute to me, as a repetition of the impropriety, this second edition, but to the demand for it.

[11] Whether he will think he has any amends made him by the following illustrations of what seemed most to require them, I myself am by no means a proper judge.

[12] There are two ways in which the subject of morals may be treated. One begins from inquiring into the abstract relations of things; the other from a matter of fact, namely, what the particular nature of man is, its several parts, their economy or constitution; from whence it proceeds to determine what course of life it is, which is correspondent to this whole nature. In the former method the conclusion is expressed thus—that vice is contrary to the nature and reason of things; in the latter, that it is a violation or breaking in upon our own nature. Thus they both lead us to the same thing, our obligations to the practice of virtue; and thus they exceedingly strengthen and enforce each other. The first seems the most direct formal proof, and in some respects the least liable to cavil and dispute; the latter is in a peculiar manner adapted to satisfy a fair mind; and is more easily applicable to the several particular relations and circumstances in life.

[13] The following discourses proceed chiefly in this latter method. The three first wholly. They were intended to explain what is meant by the nature of man, when it is said that virtue consists in following, and vice in deviating from it; and by explaining to show that the assertion is true. That the ancient moralists had some inward feeling or other, which they chose to express in this manner, that man is born to virtue, that it consists in following nature, and that vice is more contrary to this nature than tortures or death, their works in our hands are instances. Now a person who found no mystery in this way of speaking of the ancients, who, without being very explicit with himself, kept to his natural feeling, went along with them, and found within himself a full conviction that what they laid down was just and true—such an one would probably wonder to see a point in which he never perceived any difficulty, so labored as this is, in the second and third sermons; insomuch perhaps as to be at a loss for the occasion, scope, and drift of them. But it need not be thought strange that this manner of expression, though familiar with them, and, if not usually carried so far, yet not uncommon amongst ourselves, should want explaining; since there are several perceptions daily felt and spoken of, which yet it may not be very easy at first view to explicate, to distinguish from all others, and ascertain exactly what the idea or perception is. The many treatises upon the passions are a proof of this, since so many would never have undertaken to unfold their several complications, and trace and resolve them into their principles, if they had thought what they were endeavoring to show was obvious to every one who felt and talked of those passions. Thus, though there seems no ground to doubt but that

the generality of mankind have the inward perception expressed so commonly in that manner by the ancient moralists, more than to doubt whether
they have those passions; yet it appeared of use to unfold that inward conviction, and lay it open in a more explicit manner than I had seen done;
especially when there were not wanting persons who manifestly mistook
the whole thing, and so had great reason to express themselves dissatisfied
with it. A late author of great and deserved reputation says that to place
virtue in following nature, is at best a loose way of talk. And he has reason to say this if what I think he intends to express, though with great
decency, be true, that scarce any other sense can be put upon those words,
but acting as any of the several parts, without distinction, of a man's nature
happened most to incline him.[1]

[14] Whoever thinks it worth while to consider this matter thoroughly,
should begin with stating to himself exactly the idea of a system, economy,
or constitution of any particular nature, or particular anything; and he
will, I suppose, find that it is an one or a whole made up of several parts;
but yet that the several parts even considered as a whole do not complete
the idea, unless in the notion of a whole you include the relations and
respects which those parts have to each other. Every work both of nature
and of art is a system; and as every particular thing, both natural and artificial, is for some use or purpose out of and beyond itself, one may add,
to what has been already brought into the idea of a system, its conducive-
ness to this one or more ends. Let us instance in a watch—suppose the
several parts of it taken to pieces and placed apart from each other: let
a man have ever so exact a notion of these several parts, unless he con-
siders the respects and relations which they have to each other, he will
not have anything like the idea of a watch. Suppose these several parts
brought together and anyhow united: neither will he yet, be the union
ever so close, have an idea which will bear any resemblance to that of a
watch. But let him view those several parts put together, or consider them
as to be put together in the manner of a watch; let him form a notion of
the relations which those several parts have to each other—all conducive
in their respective ways to this purpose, showing the hour of the day; and
then he has the idea of a watch. Thus it is with regard to the inward frame
of man. Appetites, passions, affections, and the principle of reflection,
considered merely as the several parts of our inward nature, do not at all
give us an idea of the system or constitution of this nature, because the
constitution is formed by somewhat not yet taken into consideration,
namely, by the relations which these several parts have to each other; the
chief of which is the authority of reflection or conscience. It is from considering the relations which the several appetites and passions in the inward frame have to each other, and, above all, the supremacy of reflection
or conscience, that we get the idea of the system or constitution of human

1. *Religion of Nature delineated*, ed. 1724, p. 22. [The author of this book was
Wm. Wollaston (1659-1724).]

nature. And from the idea itself it will as fully appear that this our nature, that is, constitution, is adapted to virtue, as from the idea of a watch it appears that its nature, that is, constitution or system, is adapted to measure time. What in fact or event commonly happens is nothing to this question. Every work of art is apt to be out of order; but this is so far from being according to its system that let the disorder increase, and it will totally destroy it. This is merely by way of explanation what an economy, system, or constitution is. And thus far the cases are perfectly parallel. If we go further, there is indeed a difference, nothing to the present purpose, but too important a one ever to be omitted. A machine is inanimate and passive, but we are agents. Our constitution is put in our own power. We are charged with it; and therefore are accountable for any disorder or violation of it.

[15] Thus nothing can possibly be more contrary to nature than vice, meaning by "nature" not only the *several parts* of our internal frame, but also the *constitution of it*. Poverty and disgrace, tortures and death, are not so contrary to it. Misery and injustice are indeed equally contrary to some different parts of our nature taken singly; but injustice is moreover contrary to the whole constitution of the nature.

[16] If it be asked whether this constitution be really what those philosophers meant, and whether they would have explained themselves in this manner, the answer is the same, as if it should be asked whether a person who had often used the word "resentment," and felt the thing, would have explained this passion exactly in the same manner in which it is done in one of these discourses. As I have no doubt but that this is a true account of that passion which he referred to and intended to express by the word "resentment," so I have no doubt but that this is the true account of the ground of that conviction which they referred to when they said vice was contrary to nature. And though it should be thought that they meant no more than that vice was contrary to the higher and better part of our nature, even this implies such a constitution as I have endeavored to explain. For the very terms "higher" and "better" imply a relation or respect of parts to each other; and these relative parts, being in one and the same nature, form a constitution and are the very idea of it. They had a perception that injustice was contrary to their nature, and that pain was so also. They observed these two perceptions totally different, not in degree but in kind; and the reflecting upon each of them, as they thus stood in their nature, wrought a full intuitive conviction that more was due and of right belonged to one of these inward perceptions, than to the other; that it demanded in all cases to govern such a creature as man. So that, upon the whole, this is a fair and true account of what was the ground of their conviction, of what they intended to refer to when they said virtue consisted in following nature—a manner of speaking not loose and undeterminate, but clear and distinct, strictly just and true.

[17] Though I am persuaded the force of this conviction is felt by almost everyone, yet since, considered as an argument and put in words,

it appears somewhat abstruse, and since the connection of it is broken in the three first sermons, it may not be amiss to give the reader the whole argument here in one view.

[18] Mankind has various instincts and principles of action, as brute creatures have; some leading most directly and immediately to the good of the community, and some most directly to private good.

[19] Man has several which brutes have not, particularly, reflection or conscience, an approbation of some principles or actions, and disapprobation of others.

[20] Brutes obey their instincts or principles of action, according to certain rules; suppose the constitution of their body, and the objects around them.

[21] The generality of mankind also obey their instincts and principles, all of them; those propensions we call good, as well as the bad, according to the same rules, namely, the constitution of their body and the external circumstances which they are in. (Therefore it is not a true representation of mankind to affirm that they are wholly governed by self-love, the love of power and sensual appetites; since, as on the one hand, they are often actuated by these, without any regard to right or wrong, so, on the other, it is manifest fact that the same persons, the generality, are frequently influenced by friendship, compassion, gratitude; and even a general abhorrence of what is base, and liking of what is fair and just, takes its turn amongst the other motives of action. This is the partial inadequate notion of human nature treated of in the first discourse; and it is by this nature, if one may speak so, that the world is in fact influenced and kept in that tolerable order in which it is.)

[22] Brutes in acting according to the rules before mentioned, their bodily constitution and circumstances act suitably to their whole nature. (It is however to be distinctly noted that the reason why we affirm this is not merely that brutes in fact act so, for this alone, however universal, does not at all determine whether such course of action be correspondent to their whole nature; but the reason of the assertion is that as in acting thus they plainly act conformably to somewhat in their nature, so, from all observations we are able to make upon them, there does not appear the least ground to imagine them to have anything else in their nature which requires a different rule or course of action.)

[23] Mankind also in acting thus would act suitably to their whole nature, if no more were to be said of man's nature than what has been now said; if that, as it is a true, were also a complete, adequate account of our nature.

[24] But that is not a complete account of man's nature. Somewhat further must be brought in to give us an adequate notion of it, namely, that one of those principles of action, conscience or reflection, compared with the rest as they all stand together in the nature of man, plainly bears upon it marks of authority over all the rest, and claims the absolute direction of them all, to allow or forbid their gratification—a disapprobation of reflection being in itself a principle manifestly superior to a mere pro-

pension. And the conclusion is that to allow no more to this superior principle or part of our nature than to other parts; to let it govern and guide only occasionally in common with the rest, as its turn happens to come, from the temper and circumstances one happens to be in; this is not to act conformably to the constitution of man; neither can any human creature be said to act conformably to his constitution of nature unless he allows to that superior principle the absolute authority which is due to it. And this conclusion is abundantly confirmed from hence, that one may determine what course of action the economy of man's nature requires, without so much as knowing in what degrees of *strength* the several principles prevail or which of them have actually the greatest influence.

[25] The practical reason of insisting so much upon this natural authority of the principle of reflection or conscience is that it seems in great measure overlooked by many who are by no means the worse sort of men. It is thought sufficient to abstain from gross wickedness, and to be humane and kind to such as happen to come in their way. Whereas in reality the very constitution of our nature requires that we bring our whole conduct before this superior faculty, wait its determination, enforce upon ourselves its authority, and make it the business of our lives, as it is absolutely the whole business of a moral agent to conform ourselves to it. This is the true meaning of that ancient precept, *reverence thyself*.

[26] The not taking into consideration this authority, which is implied in the idea of reflex approbation or disapprobation, seems a material deficiency or omission in Lord Shaftesbury's inquiry concerning virtue. He has shown beyond all contradiction, that virtue is naturally the interest or happiness, and vice the misery, of such a creature as man, placed in the circumstances which we are in this world. But suppose there are particular exceptions, a case which this author was unwilling to put, and yet surely it is to be put; or suppose a case which he has put and determined, that of a sceptic not convinced of this happy tendency of virtue, or being of a contrary opinion. His determination is, that it would be *without remedy*.[2] One may say more explicitly, that leaving out the authority of reflex approbation or disapprobation, such an one would be under an obligation to act viciously; since interest, one's own happiness, is a manifest obligation, and there is not supposed to be any other obligation in the case. "But does it much mend the matter, to take in that natural authority of reflection? There indeed would be an obligation to virtue; but would not the obligation from supposed interest on the side of vice remain?" If it should, yet to be under two contrary obligations, i.e. under none at all, would not be exactly the same, as to be under a formal obligation to be vicious, or to be in circumstances in which the constitution of man's nature plainly required that vice should be preferred. But the obligation on the side of interest really does not remain. For the natural authority of the principle of reflection is an obligation the most near and intimate, the most certain and known; whereas the contrary obligation can at the utmost appear no

2. *Characteristics* (ed., 1727), ii, p. 69.

more than probable, since no man can be *certain* in any circumstances that vice is his interest in the present world, much less can he be certain against another; and thus the certain obligation would entirely supersede and destroy the uncertain one; which yet would have been of real force without the former.

[27] In truth, the taking in this consideration totally changes the whole state of the case, and shows, what this author does not seem to have been aware of, that the greatest degree of scepticism which he thought possible will still leave men under the strictest moral obligations, whatever their opinion be concerning the happiness of virtue. For that mankind upon reflection felt an approbation of what was good, and disapprobation of the contrary, he thought a plain matter of fact, as it undoubtedly is, which none could deny, but from mere affectation. Take in then that authority and obligation, which is a constituent part of this reflex approbation, and it will undeniably follow, though a man should doubt of everything else, yet, that he would still remain under the nearest and most certain obligation to the practice of virtue, an obligation implied in the very idea of virtue, in the very idea of reflex approbation.

[28] And how little influence soever this obligation alone can be expected to have in fact upon mankind, yet one may appeal even to interest and self-love, and ask, since for man's nature, condition, and the shortness of life, so little, so very little indeed, can possibly in any case be gained by vice, whether it be so prodigious a thing to sacrifice that little to the most intimate of all obligations, and which a man cannot transgress without being self-condemned, and, unless he has corrupted his nature, without real self-dislike; this question, I say, may be asked, even upon supposition that the prospect of a future life were ever so uncertain.

[29] The observation, that man is thus by his very nature a law to himself, pursued to its just consequences, is of the utmost importance; because from it it will follow, that though men should, through stupidity or speculative scepticism, be ignorant of, or disbelieve, any authority in the universe to punish the violation of this law, yet, if there should be such authority, they would be as really liable to punishment, as though they had been beforehand convinced that such punishment would follow. For in whatever sense we understand justice, even supposing, what I think would be very presumptuous to assert, that the end of Divine punishment is no other than that of civil punishment, namely, to prevent future mischief, upon this bold supposition, ignorance or disbelief of the sanction would by no means exempt even from this justice; because it is not foreknowledge of the punishment which renders us obnoxious to it, but merely violating a known obligation.

.   .   .   .

[35] The chief design of the eleventh discourse is to state the notion of self-love and disinterestedness, in order to show that benevolence is not more unfriendly to self-love than any other particular affection whatever.

There is a strange affectation in many people of explaining away all particular affections, and representing the whole of life as nothing but one
continued exercise of self-love. Hence arises that surprising confusion and
perplexity in the Epicureans[3] of old, Hobbes, the author of *Reflexions,
Sentences, et Maximes Morales,*[4] and this whole set of writers—the confusion of calling actions interested which are done in contradiction to the
most manifest known interest, merely for the gratification of a present
passion. Now all this confusion might easily be avoided, by stating to ourselves wherein the idea of self-love in general consists, as distinguished
from all particular movements toward particular external objects—the
appetites of sense, resentment, compassion, curiosity, ambition, and the
rest.[5] When this is done, if the words "selfish" and "interested" cannot
be parted with but must be applied to everything, yet, to avoid such total
confusion of all language, let the distinction be made by epithets: and the
first may be called cool or settled selfishness, and the other passionate or
sensual selfishness. But the most natural way of speaking plainly is to call
the first only "self-love," and the actions proceeding from it "interested";
and to say of the latter that they are not love to ourselves, but movements
toward somewhat external: honor, power, the harm or good of another;
and that the pursuit of these external objects, so far as it proceeds from
these movements (for it may proceed from self-love),[6] is no otherwise
interested than as every action of every creature must, from the nature of
the thing, be; for no one can act but from a desire or choice or preference
of his own.

[36] Self-love and any particular passion may be joined together; and
from this complication it becomes impossible in numberless instances to
determine precisely how far an action, perhaps even of one's own, has for
its principle general self-love or some particular passion. But this need
create no confusion in the ideas themselves of self-love and particular
passions. We distinctly discern what one is and what the others are, though
we may be uncertain how far one or the other influences us. And though,
from this uncertainty, it cannot but be that there will be different opinions
concerning mankind as more or less governed by interest, and some will
ascribe actions to self-love, which others will ascribe to particular pas-

3. One need only look into Torquatus's account of the Epicurean system, in
Cicero's first book *de Finibus,* to see in what a surprising manner this was done by
them. Thus the desire of praise, and of being beloved, he explains to be no other than
desire of safety; regard to our country, even in the most virtuous character, to be
nothing but regard to ourselves [*de Fin.* i. 10]. The author of *Reflexions, etc., Morales,* says, "Curiosity proceeds from interest or pride; which pride also would doubtless have been explained to be self-love" (page 85, ed. 1725). As if there were no
such passions in mankind as desire of esteem, or of being beloved, or of knowledge.
Hobbes's account of the affections of goodwill and pity are instances of the same kind.

4. [That is, the Duke de la Rochefoucauld (1613-1680).]

5. Serm. XI. 5ff. [Serm. IV. 5 in this edition.—Ed.]

6. See Serm. I. 6 note.

sions; yet it is absurd to say that mankind are wholly actuated by either, since it is manifest that both have their influence. For as, on the one hand, men form a general notion of interest, some placing it in one thing, and some in another, and have a considerable regard to it throughout the course of their life, which is owing to self-love; so, on the other hand, they are often set on work by the particular passions themselves, and a considerable part of life is spent in the actual gratification of them, that is, is employed, not by self-love, but by the passions.

[37] Besides, the very idea of an interested pursuit necessarily presupposes particular passions or appetites, since the very idea of interest or happiness consists in this that an appetite or affection enjoys its object. It is not because we love ourselves that we find delight in such and such objects, but because we have particular affections toward them. Take away these affections and you leave self-love absolutely nothing at all to employ itself about;[7] no end or object for it to pursue except only that of avoiding pain. Indeed, the Epicureans, who maintained that absence of pain was the highest happiness, might, consistently with themselves, deny all affection and, if they had so pleased, every sensual appetite, too; but the very idea of interest or happiness other than absence of pain implies particular appetites or passions, these being necessary to constitute that interest or happiness.

[38] The observation that benevolence is no more distinterested than any of the common particular passions,[8] seems in itself worth being taken notice of; but is insisted upon to obviate that scorn which one sees rising upon the faces of people who are said to know the world, when mention is made of a disinterested, generous, or public-spirited action. The truth of that observation might be made appear in a more formal manner of proof; for whoever will consider all the possible respects and relations which any particular affection can have to self-love and private interest, will, I think, see demonstrably that benevolence is not in any respect more at variance with self-love than any other particular affection whatever, but that it is in every respect, at least, as friendly to it.

[39] If the observation be true, it follows that self-love and benevolence, virtue and interest, are not to be opposed but only to be distinguished from each other, in the same way as virtue and any other particular affection, love of arts, suppose, are to be distinguished. Everything is what it is, and not another thing. The goodness or badness of actions does not arise from hence that the epithet "interested" or "disinterested" may be applied to them, any more than that any other indifferent epithet, suppose "inquisitive" or "jealous," may or may not be applied to them, not from their being attended with present or future pleasure or pain, but from their being what they are, namely, what becomes such creatures as

7. Serm. XI. 9. [Serm. IV. 9 in this edition.—Ed.]

8. Serm. XI. 11. [Serm. IV. 11 in this edition.—Ed.]

we are, what the state of the case requires, or the contrary. Or in other words, we may judge and determine that an action is morally good or evil before we so much as consider whether it be interested or disinterested. This consideration no more comes in to determine whether an action be virtuous than to determine whether it be resentful. Self-love in its due degree is as just and morally good as any affection whatever. Benevolence toward particular persons may be to a degree of weakness, and so be blamable; and disinterestedness is so far from being in itself commendable that the utmost possible depravity which we can in imagination conceive is that of disinterested cruelty.

[40] Neither does there appear any reason to wish self-love were weaker in the generality of the world than it is. The influence which it has seems plainly owing to its being constant and habitual, which it cannot but be, and not to the degree or strength of it. Every caprice of the imagination, every curiosity of the understanding, every affection of the heart is perpetually showing its weakness, by prevailing over it. Men daily, hourly sacrifice the greatest known interest to fancy, inquisitiveness, love, or hatred, any vagrant inclination. The thing to be lamented is not that men have so great regard to their own good or interest in the present world, for they have not enough;[9] but that they have so little to the good of others. And this seems plainly owing to their being so much engaged in the gratification of particular passions unfriendly to benevolence, and which happen to be most prevalent in them, much more than to self-love. As a proof of this may be observed that there is no character more void of friendship, gratitude, natural affection, love to their country, common justice, or more equally and uniformly hard-hearted, than the *abandoned* in, what is called, the way of pleasure—hard-hearted and totally without feeling in behalf of others except when they cannot escape the sight of distress, and so are interrupted by it in their pleasures. And yet it is ridiculous to call such an abandoned course of pleasure interested when the person engaged in it knows beforehand, and goes on under the feeling and apprehension, that it will be as ruinous to himself as to those who depend upon him.

[41] Upon the whole, if the generality of mankind were to cultivate within themselves the principle of self-love, if they were to accustom themselves often to set down and consider what was the greatest happiness they were capable of attaining for themselves in this life, and if self-love were so strong and prevalent as that they would uniformly pursue this their supposed chief temporal good, without being diverted from it by any particular passion, it would manifestly prevent numberless follies and vices. This was in a great measure the Epicurean system of philosophy. It is indeed by no means the religious or even moral institution of life. Yet, with all the mistakes men would fall into about interest, it would be less mischievous than the extravagances of mere appetite, will, and pleasure; for certainly self-love, though confined to the interest of this life, is, of

9. Serm. I. 14.

the two, a much better guide than passion,[10] which has absolutely no bound nor measure but what is set to it by this self-love or moral considerations.

[42] From the distinction above made between self-love and the several particular principles or affections in our nature, we may see how good ground there was for that assertion, maintained by the several ancient schools of philosophy against the Epicureans, namely, that virtue is to be pursued as an end, eligible in and for itself. For, if there be any principles or affections in the mind of man distinct from self-love, that the things those principles tend towards, or that the objects of those affections are, each of them, in themselves eligible, to be pursued upon its own account, and to be rested in as an end, is implied in the very idea of such principle or affection.[11] They indeed asserted much higher things of virtue, and with very good reason; but to say thus much of it, that it is to be pursued for itself, is to say no more of it than may truly be said of the object of every natural affection whatever.

[43] The question which was a few years ago disputed in France, concerning *the love of God,* which was there called "enthusiasm," as it will everywhere by the generality of the world—this question, I say, answers in religion to that old one in morals now mentioned. And both of them are, I think, fully determined by the same observation, namely, that the very nature of affection, the idea itself, necessarily implies resting in its object as an end.

[44] I shall not here add anything further to what I have said in the two discourses upon that most important subject, but only this—that if we are constituted such sort of creatures, as from our very nature to feel certain affections or movements of mind, upon the sight or contemplation of the meanest inanimate part of the creation, for the flowers of the field have their beauty; certainly there must be somewhat due to Himself, who is the author and cause of all things, who is more intimately present to us than anything else can be, and with whom we have a nearer and more constant intercourse than we can have with any creature; there must be some movements of mind and heart which correspond to His perfections, or of which those perfections are the natural object; and that when we are commanded to "love the Lord our God with all our heart, and with all our mind, and with all our soul"[12] somewhat more must be meant than merely that we live in hope of rewards or fear of punishments from Him; somewhat more than this must be intended, though these regards themselves are most just and reasonable, and absolutely necessary to be often recollected in such a world as this.

[45] It may be proper just to advertise the reader that he is not to look for any particular reason for the choice of the greatest part of these dis-

10. Serm. II. 25.

11. Serm. XIII. 5.

12. [*St. Matt.* XXII: 37.]

courses, their being taken from amongst many others, preached in the same place, through a course of eight years, being in great measure accidental. Neither is he to expect to find any other connection between them than that uniformity of thought and design which will always be found in the writings of the same person when he writes with simplicity and in earnest.

STANHOPE, *September* 16, 1729.

SERMON I

UPON HUMAN NATURE

For as we have many members in one body, and all members have not the same office: so we, being many, are one body in Christ, and every one members one of another (Romans XII: 4, 5).

[1] THE EPISTLES in the New Testament have all of them a particular reference to the condition and usages of the Christian world at the time they were written. Therefore, as they cannot be thoroughly understood unless that condition and those usages are known and attended to, so further, though they be known, yet if they be discontinued or changed, exhortations, precepts, and illustrations of things, which refer to such circumstances now ceased or altered, cannot at this time be urged in that manner and with that force which they were to the primitive Christians. Thus the text now before us, in its first intent and design, relates to the decent management of those extraordinary gifts which were then in the church,[1] but which are now totally ceased. And even as to the allusion that "we are one body in Christ," though what the apostle here intends is equally true of Christians in all circumstances—and the consideration of it is plainly still an additional motive, over and above moral considerations, to the discharge of the several duties and offices of a Christian—yet it is manifest this allusion must have appeared with much greater force to those who, by the many difficulties they went through for the sake of their religion, were led to keep always in view the relation they stood in to their Saviour, who had undergone the same; to those who, from the idolatries of all around them and their ill treatment, were taught to consider themselves as not of the world in which they lived, but as a distinct society of themselves, with laws and ends, and principles of life and action, quite contrary to those which the world professed themselves at that time influenced by. Hence the relation of a Christian was by them considered as nearer than that of affinity and blood; and they almost literally esteemed themselves as members one of another.

[2] It cannot indeed possibly be denied that our being God's creatures, and virtue being the natural law we are born under, and the whole constitution of man being plainly adapted to it, are prior obligations to piety and virtue than the consideration that God sent his Son into the world to save it, and the motives which arise from the peculiar relations of Christians, as members one of another under Christ our Head. However, though all this be allowed, as it expressly is by the inspired writers, yet it is manifest that Christians at the time of the revelation, and immediately after, could not but insist mostly upon considerations of this latter kind.

1. *I Cor.* XII.

25

[3] These observations show the original particular reference of the text; and the peculiar force with which the thing intended by the allusion in it, must have been felt by the primitive Christian world. They likewise afford a reason for treating it at this time in a more general way.

[4] The relation which the several parts or members of the natural body have to each other and to the whole body is here compared to the relation which each particular person in society has to other particular persons and to the whole society; and the latter is intended to be illustrated by the former. And if there be a likeness between these two relations, the consequence is obvious: that the latter shows us [we were intended]² to to do good to others, as the former shows us that [the several members of the natural body were intended to be instruments of good to each other and the whole body].³ But as there is scarce any ground for a comparison between society and the mere material body, this without the mind being a dead unactive thing, much less can the comparison be carried to any length. And since the apostle speaks of the several members as having distinct offices, which implies the mind, it cannot be thought an unallowable liberty, instead of the *body* and *its members,* to substitute the *whole nature of man* and *all the variety of internal principles which belong to it.* And then the comparison will be between the nature of man as respecting self and tending to private good, his own preservation and happiness, and the nature of man as having respect to society and tending to promote public good, the happiness of that society. These ends do indeed perfectly coincide; and to aim at public and private good are so far from being inconsistent that they mutually promote each other; yet in the following discourse they must be considered as entirely distinct, otherwise the nature of man as tending to one, or as tending to the other, cannot be compared. There can no comparison be made without considering the things compared as distinct and different.

[5] From this review and comparison of the nature of man as respecting self and as respecting society, it will plainly appear that there are as real and the same kind of indications in human nature that we were made for society and to do good to our fellow creatures, as that we were intended to take care of our own life and health and private good; and that the same objections lie against one of these assertions as against the other. For,

[6] First, there is a natural principle of *benevolence*⁴ in man, which is in some degree to *society* what *self-love* is to the *individual.* And if

2. [Ed. I. has "it is our duty."]

3. [Ed. I. has "we are to take care of our own private interest," an apparent slip, for the analogy does not establish this of itself.]

4. Suppose a man of learning to be writing a grave book upon *human nature,* and to show in several parts of it that he had an insight into the subject he was considering; amongst other things, the following one would require to be accounted for: the appearance of benevolence or goodwill in men toward each other in the instances of natural relation, and in others (Hobbes, *Of Human Nature,* c. ix. § 7). Cautious of

there be in mankind any disposition to friendship; if there be any such thing as compassion, for compassion is momentary love; if there be any such thing as the paternal or filial affections; if there be any affection in human nature the object and end of which is the good of another—this is itself benevolence or the love of another. Be it ever so short, be it in ever so low a degree, or ever so unhappily confined, it proves the assertion and points out what we were designed for, as really as though it were in a higher degree and more extensive. I must however remind you that though benevolence and self-love are different, though the former tends most directly to public good, and the latter to private, yet they are so perfectly coincident that the greatest satisfactions to ourselves depend upon our having benevolence in a due degree, and that self-love is one chief security of our right behavior toward society. It may be added that their mutual coinciding, so that we can scarce promote one without the other, is equally a proof that we were made for both.

---

being deceived with outward show, he retires within himself to see exactly what that is in the mind of man from whence this appearance proceeds; and, upon deep reflection, asserts the principle in the mind to be only the love of power, and delight in the exercise of it. Would not everybody think here was a mistake of one word for another; that the philosopher was contemplating and accounting for some other human actions, some other behavior of man to man? And could anyone be thoroughly satisfied that what is commonly called benevolence or goodwill was really the affection meant, but only by being made to understand that this learned person had a general hypothesis to which the appearance of goodwill could no otherwise be reconciled? That what has this appearance is often nothing but ambition; that delight in superiority often (suppose always) mixes itself with benevolence, only makes it more specious to call it ambition than hunger, of the two: but in reality that passion does no more account for the whole appearances of goodwill than this appetite does. Is there not often the appearance of one man's wishing that good to another which he knows himself unable to procure him; and rejoicing in it, though bestowed by a third person? And can love of power anyway possibly come in to account for this desire or delight? Is there not often the appearance of men's distinguishing between two or more persons, preferring one before another, to do good to, in cases where love of power cannot in the least account for the distinction and preference? For this principle can no otherwise distinguish between objects than as it is a greater instance and exertion of power to do good to one rather than to another. Again, suppose goodwill in the mind of man to be nothing but delight in the exercise of power; men might indeed be restrained by distant and accidental considerations; but these restraints being removed, they would have a disposition to, and delight in, mischief as an exercise and proof of power: and this disposition and delight would arise from or be the same principle in the mind, as a disposition to, and delight in, charity. Thus cruelty, as distinct from envy and resentment, would be exactly the same in the mind of man as goodwill—that one tends to the happiness, the other to the misery of our fellow creatures, is, it seems, merely an accidental circumstance, which the mind has not the least regard to. These are the absurdities which even men of capacity run into when they have occasion to belie their nature, and will perversely disclaim that image of God which was originally stamped upon it, the traces of which, however faint, are plainly discernible upon the mind of man.

If any person can in earnest doubt whether there be such a thing as goodwill in one man toward another (for the question is not concerning either the degree or extensiveness of it, but concerning the affection itself), let it be observed that whether man be thus or otherwise constituted, what is the inward frame in this

[7] Secondly, this will further appear, from observing that the *several passions and affections,* which are distinct[5] both from benevolence and self-love, do in general contribute and lead us to *public* good as really as to *private.* It might be thought too minute and particular, and would carry us too great a length, to distinguish between and compare together the several passions or appetites distinct from benevolence, whose primary use and intention is the security and good of society; and the passions

---

particular, is a mere question of fact or natural history, not provable immediately by reason. It is therefore to be judged of and determined in the same way other facts or matters of natural history are: by appealing to the external senses or inward perceptions respectively, as the matter under consideration is cognizable by one or the other; by arguing from acknowledged facts and actions; for a great number of actions in the same kind, in different circumstances, and respecting different objects, will prove, to a certainty, what principles they do not, and, to the greatest probability, what principles they do proceed from; and lastly, by the testimony of mankind. Now that there is some degree of benevolence amongst men may be as strongly and plainly proved in all these ways, as it could possibly be proved, supposing there was this affection in our nature. And should anyone think fit to assert that resentment in the mind of man was absolutely nothing but reasonable concern for our own safety, the falsity of this, and what is the real nature of that passion, could be shown in no other ways than those in which it may be shown, that there is such a thing in some degree as real goodwill in man toward man. It is sufficient that the seeds of it be implanted in our nature by God. There is, it is owned, much left for us to do upon our own heart and temper; to cultivate, to improve, to call it forth, to exercise it in a steady, uniform manner. This is our work; this is virtue and religion.

5. Everybody makes a distinction between self-love and the several particular passions, appetites, and affections; and yet they are often confounded again. That they are totally different, will be seen by any one who will distinguish between the passions and appetites themselves, and endeavoring after the means of their gratification. Consider the appetite of hunger, and the desire of esteem; these being the occasion both of pleasure and pain, the coolest self-love, as well as the appetites and passions themselves, may put us upon making use of the proper methods of obtaining that pleasure, and avoiding that pain; but the feelings themselves, the pain of hunger and shame, and the delight from esteem, are no more self-love than they are anything in the world. Though a man hated himself, he would as much feel the pain of hunger as he would that of the gout; and it is plainly supposable there may be creatures with self-love in them to the highest degree, who may be quite insensible and indifferent (as men in some cases are) to the contempt and esteem of those upon whom their happiness does not in some further respects depend. And as self-love and the several particular passions and appetites are in themselves totally different, so that some actions proceed from one, and some from the other, will be manifest to any who will observe the two following very supposable cases. One man rushes upon certain ruin for the gratification of a present desire; nobody will call the principle of this action self-love. Suppose another man to go through some laborious work upon promise of a great reward, without any distinct knowledge what the reward will be; this course of action cannot be ascribed to any particular passion. The former of these actions is plainly to be imputed to some particular passion or affection, the latter as plainly to the general affection or principle of self-love. That there are some particular pursuits or actions concerning which we cannot determine how far they are owing to one, and how far to the other, proceeds from this that the two principles are frequently mixed together, and run up into each other. This distinction is further explained in the eleventh sermon [Sermon IV in this edition.—Ed.]

distinct from self-love, whose primary intention and design is the security and good of the individual.[6] It is enough to the present argument that desire of esteem from others, contempt and esteem of them, love of society as distinct from affection to the good of it, indignation against successful vice—that these are public affections or passions, have an immediate respect to others, naturally lead us to regulate our behavior in such a manner as will be of service to our fellow creatures. If any or all of these may be considered likewise as private affections, as tending to private good, this does not hinder them from being public affections, too, or destroy the good influence of them upon society, and their tendency to public good. It may be added that as persons without any conviction from reason of the desirableness of life would yet of course preserve it merely from the appetite of hunger, so by acting merely from regard (suppose) to reputation, without any consideration of the good of others, men often contribute to public good. In both these instances they are plainly instruments in the hands of another, in the hands of Providence, to carry on ends, the preservation of the individual and good of society, which they themselves have not in their view or intention. The sum is, men have various appetites, passions, and particular affections, quite distinct both from self-love and from benevolence—all of these have a tendency to promote both public and private good, and may be considered as respecting others and ourselves equally and in common; but some of them seem most immediately to respect others, or tend to public good, others of them most immediately to respect self, or tend to private good; as the former are not benevolence, so the latter are not self-love; neither sort are instances of our love either to ourselves or others, but only instances of our Maker's care and love both of the individual and the species, and proofs that He intended we should be instruments of good to each other, as well as that we should be so to ourselves.

[8] Thirdly, there is a principle of reflection in men by which they distinguish between, approve and disapprove, their own actions. We are plainly constituted such sort of creatures as to reflect upon our own nature. The mind can take a view of what passes within itself, its propensions, aversions, passions, affections, as respecting such objects and in such degrees, and of the several actions consequent thereupon. In this survey it approves of one, disapproves of another, and toward a third is affected in neither of these ways, but is quite indifferent. This principle

6. If any desire to see this distinction and comparison made in a particular instance, the appetite and passion now mentioned may serve for one. Hunger is to be considered as a private appetite; because the end for which it was given us is the preservation of the individual. Desire of esteem is a public passion; because the end for which it was given us is to regulate our behavior toward society. The respect which this has to private good is as remote as the respect that has to public good: and the appetite is no more self-love than the passion is benevolence. The object and end of the former is merely food; the object and end of the latter is merely esteem; but the latter can no more be gratified without contributing to the good of society, than the former can be gratified without contributing to the preservation of the individual.

in man by which he approves or disapproves his heart, temper, and actions, is conscience [for this is the strict sense of the word, though sometimes it is used so as to take in more].[7] And that this faculty tends to
restrain men from doing mischief to each other, and leads them to do
good, is too manifest to need being insisted upon. Thus a parent has
the affection of love to his children; this leads him to take care of, to
educate, to make due provision for them; the natural affection leads to
this, but the reflection that it is his proper business, what belongs to him,
that it is right and commendable so to do—this added to the affection
becomes a much more settled principle and carries him on through more
labor and difficulties for the sake of his children than he would undergo
from that affection alone, if he thought it, and the course of action it led
to, either indifferent or criminal. This indeed is impossible, to do that
which is good and not to approve of it; for which reason they are frequently not considered as distinct, though they really are, for men often
approve of the actions of others which they will not imitate, and likewise do that which they approve not. It cannot possibly be denied that
there is this principle of reflection or conscience in human nature. Suppose
a man to relieve an innocent person in great distress, suppose the same
man afterwards, in the fury of anger, to do the greatest mischief to a
person who had given no just cause of offense; to aggravate the injury,
add the circumstances of former friendship and obligation from the in-
jured person, let the man who is supposed to have done these two different
actions coolly reflect upon them afterwards, without regard to their consequences to himself; to assert that any common man would be affected
in the same way toward these different actions, that he would make no
distinction between them, but approve or disapprove them equally, is
too glaring a falsity to need being confuted. There is therefore this principle of reflection or conscience in mankind. It is needless to compare
the respect it has to private good with the respect it has to public, since
it plainly tends as much to the latter as to the former, and is commonly
thought to tend chiefly to the latter. This faculty is now mentioned merely
as another part in the inward frame of man, pointing out to us in some
degree what we are intended for, and as what will naturally and of course
have some influence. The particular place assigned to it by nature, what
authority it has, and how great influence it ought to have, shall be hereafter considered.

[9] From this comparison of benevolence and self-love, of our public
and private affections, of the courses of life they lead to, and of the principle of reflection or conscience as respecting each of them, it is as manifest that we were made for society and to promote the happiness of it,
as that we were intended to take care of our own life and health and
private good.

[10] And from this whole review must be given a different draught
of human nature from what we are often presented with. Mankind are by

7. [Ed. I. has "which word is used in different senses, but often in this."]

nature so closely united, there is such a correspondence between the inward sensations of one man and those of another that disgrace is as much avoided as bodily pain, and to be the object of esteem and love as much desired as any external goods; and in many particular cases, persons are carried on to do good to others, as the end their affection tends to and rests in, and manifest that they find real satisfaction and enjoyment in this course of behavior. There is such a natural principle of attraction in man toward man that having trod the same tract of land, having breathed in the same climate, barely having been born in the same artificial district or division, becomes the occasion of contracting acquaintances and familiarities many years after; for anything may serve the purpose. Thus relations merely nominal are sought and invented, not by governors, but by the lowest of the people; which are found sufficient to hold mankind together in little fraternities and copartnerships—weak ties indeed, and what may afford fund enough for ridicule if they are absurdly considered as the real principles of that union; but they are in truth merely the occasions, as anything may be of anything, upon which our nature carries us on according to its own previous bent and bias; which occasions therefore would be nothing at all were there not this prior disposition and bias of nature. Men are so much one body that in a peculiar manner they feel for each other; shame, sudden danger, resentment, honor, prosperity, distress; one or another, or all of these, from the social nature in general, from benevolence, upon the occasion of natural relation, acquaintance, protection, dependence—each of these being distinct cements of society. And therefore to have no restraint from, no regard to, others in our behavior is the speculative absurdity of considering ourselves as single and independent, as having nothing in our nature which has respect to our fellow creatures, reduced to action and practice. And this is the same absurdity as to suppose a hand or any part to have no natural respect to any other or to the whole body.

[11] But allowing all this, it may be asked, "Has not man dispositions and principles within, which lead him to do evil to others as well as to do good? Whence come the many miseries else, which men are the authors and instruments of to each other?" These questions, so far as they relate to the foregoing discourse, may be answered by asking, Has not man also dispositions and principles within, which lead him to do evil to himself as well as good? Whence come the many miseries else, sickness, pain, and death, which men are instruments and authors of to themselves?

[12] It may be thought more easy to answer one of these questions than the other, but the answer to both is really the same—that mankind have ungoverned passions which they will gratify at any rate, as well to the injury of others as in contradiction to known private interest, but that as there is no such thing as self-hatred, so neither is there any such thing as ill-will in one man toward another, emulation and resentment being away, whereas there is plainly benevolence or good-will; there is no such thing as love of injustice, oppression, treachery, ingratitude, but only eager desires after such and such external goods, which, according

to a very ancient observation, the most abandoned would choose to obtain by innocent means if they were as easy and as effectual to their end that even emulation and resentment, by any one who will consider what these passions really are in nature,[8] will be found nothing to the purpose of this objection; and that the principles and passions in the mind of man, which are distinct both from self-love and benevolence, primarily and most directly lead to right behavior with regard to others as well as himself, and only secondarily and accidentally to what is evil. Thus, though men, to avoid the shame of one villainy, are sometimes guilty of a greater, yet it is easy to see that the original tendency of shame is to prevent the doing of shameful actions; and its leading men to conceal such actions when done is only in consequence of their being done, that is, of the passion's not having answered its first end.

[13] If it be said that there are persons in the world who are in great measure without the natural affections toward their fellow creatures, there are likewise instances of persons without the common natural affections to themselves; but the nature of man is not to be judged of by either of these, but by what appears in the common world, in the bulk of mankind.

[14] I am afraid it would be thought very strange if to confirm the truth of this account of human nature and make out the justness of the foregoing comparison, it should be added that, from what appears, men in fact as much and as often contradict that *part* of their nature which respects *self* and which leads them to their *own private* good and happiness, as they contradict that *part* of it which respects *society* and tends to *public* good; that there are as few persons who attain the greatest satisfaction and enjoyment which they might attain in the present world, as who do the greatest good to others which they might do—nay, that there are as few who can be said really and in earnest to aim at one as at the other. Take a survey of mankind: the world in general, the good and bad, almost without exception, equally are agreed that were religion out of the case, the happiness of the present life would consist in a manner wholly in riches, honors, sensual gratifications, insomuch that one scarce hears a reflection made upon prudence, life, conduct, but upon this supposition. Yet on the contrary, that persons in the greatest affluence of fortune are no happier than such as have only a competency; that the cares and disappointments of ambition for the most part far exceed the satisfactions of it; as also the miserable intervals of intemperance and excess, and the many untimely deaths occasioned by a dissolute course of life—

---

8. Emulation is merely the desire and hope of equality with, or superiority over, others with whom we compare ourselves. There does not appear to be any other grief in the natural passion, but only that want which is implied in desire. However, this may be so strong as to be the occasion of great grief. To desire the attainment of this equality or superiority by the particular means of others being brought down to our own level, or below it, is, I think, the distinct notion of envy. From whence it is easy to see that the real end, which the natural passion, emulation, and which the unlawful one, envy, aims at, is exactly the same—namely, that equality or superiority and consequently that to do mischief is not the end of envy, but merely the means it makes use of to attain its end. As to resentment, see the eighth sermon.

these things are all seen, acknowledged, by every one acknowledged, but are thought no objections against, though they expressly contradict this universal principle that the happiness of the present life consists in one or other of them. Whence is all this absurdity and contradiction? Is not the middle way obvious? Can anything be more manifest than that the happiness of life consists in these possessed and enjoyed only to a certain degree, that to pursue them beyond this degree is always attended with more inconvenience than advantage to a man's self, and often with extreme misery and unhappiness? Whence then, I say, is all this absurdity and contradiction? Is it really the result of consideration in mankind how they may become most easy to themselves, most free from care, and enjoy the chief happiness attainable in this world? Or is it not manifestly owing either to this that they have not cool and reasonable concern enough for themselves to consider wherein their chief happiness in the present life consists, or else, if they do consider it, that they will not act conformably to what is the result of that consideration; that is, reasonable concern for themselves, or cool self-love, is prevailed over by passion and appetite. So that, from what appears, there is no ground to assert [that those principles in the nature of man which most directly lead to promote the good of our fellow creatures are more generally or in a greater degree violated than those which most directly lead us to promote our own private good and happiness.][9]

[15] The sum of the whole is plainly this. The nature of man considered in his single capacity, and with respect only to the present world, is adapted and leads him to attain the greatest happiness he can for himself in the present world. The nature of man considered in his public or social capacity leads him to a right behavior in society, to that course of life which we call virtue. Men follow or obey their nature in both these capacities and respects to a certain degree, but not entirely; their actions do not come up to the whole of what their nature leads them to in either of these capacities or respects; and they often violate their nature in both. That is, as they neglect the duties they owe to their fellow creatures, to which their nature leads them, and are injurious, to which their nature is abhorrent, so there is a manifest negligence in men of their real happiness or interest in the present world when that interest is inconsistent with a present gratification, for the sake of which they negligently, nay, even knowingly, are the authors and instruments of their own misery and ruin. Thus they are as often unjust to themselves as to others, and for the most part are equally so to both by the same actions.

9. [Ed. I. has "that cool self-love has any more influence upon the actions of men than the principles of virtue and benevolence have," a statement which is much more open to dispute than the corrected statement in the text.]

SERMON II

UPON HUMAN NATURE

For when the Gentiles, which have not the law, do by nature the things contained in the law, these, having not the law, are a law unto themselves (Romans II: 14).

[1] AS SPECULATIVE TRUTH admits of different kinds of proof, so likewise moral obligations may be shown by different methods. If the real nature of any creature leads him and is adapted to such and such purposes only, or more than to any other, this is a reason to believe the Author of that nature intended it for those purposes. Thus there is no doubt the eye was intended for us to see with. And the more complex any constitution is, and the greater variety of parts there are which thus tend to some one end, the stronger is the proof that such end was designed. However, when the inward frame of man is considered as any guide in morals, the utmost caution must be used that none make peculiarities in their own temper, or anything which is the effect of particular customs, though observable in several, the standard of what is common to the species; and above all, that the highest principle be not forgotten or excluded, that to which belongs the adjustment and correction of all other inward movements and affections; which principle will of course have some influence, but which being in nature supreme, as shall now be shown, ought to preside over and govern all the rest. The difficulty of rightly observing the two former cautions, the appearance there is of some small diversity amongst mankind with respect to this faculty, with respect to their natural sense of moral good and evil, and the attention necessary to survey with any exactness what passes within, have occasioned that it is not so much agreed what is the standard of the internal nature of man as of his external form. Neither is this last exactly settled. Yet we understand one another when we speak of the shape of a human body; so likewise we do when we speak of the heart and inward principles, how far soever the standard is from being exact or precisely fixed. There is therefore ground for an attempt of showing men to themselves, of showing them what course of life and behavior their real nature points out and would lead them to. Now obligations of virtue shown, and motives to the practice of it enforced, from a review of the nature of man, are to be considered as an appeal to each particular person's heart and natural conscience, as the external senses are appealed to for the proof of things cognizable by them. Since then our inward feelings, and the perceptions we receive from our external senses, are equally real; to argue from the former to life and conduct is as little liable to exception as to argue from the latter to absolute speculative truth. A man can as little doubt whether his eyes were given him to see with, as he can doubt of the truth of the science of *optics* deduced from ocular experiments. And allowing the inward feeling, shame, a man can

as little doubt whether it was given him to prevent his doing shameful actions, as he can doubt whether his eyes were given him to guide his steps. And as to these inward feelings themselves—that they are real, that man has in his nature passions and affections, can no more be questioned than that he has external senses. Neither can the former be wholly mistaken, though to a certain degree liable to greater mistakes than the latter.

[2] There can be no doubt but that several propensions or instincts, several principles in the heart of man, carry him to society, and to contribute to the happiness of it, in a sense and a manner in which no inward principle leads him to evil. These principles, propensions, or instincts which lead him to do good are approved of by a certain faculty within, quite distinct from these propensions themselves. All this hath been fully made out in the foregoing discourse.

[3] But it may be said, "What is all this, though true, to the purpose of virtue and religion? These require not only that we do good to others, when we are led this way by benevolence or reflection happening to be stronger than other principles, passions, or appetites, but likewise that the *whole* character be formed upon thought and reflection, that *every* action be directed by some determinate rule, some other rule than the strength and prevalency of any principle or passion. What sign is there in our nature (for the inquiry is only about what is to be collected from thence) that this was intended by its Author? Or how does so various and fickle a temper as that of man appear adapted thereto? It may indeed be absurd and unnatural for men to act without any reflection, nay, without regard to that particular kind of reflection which you call conscience; because this does belong to our nature. For as there never was a man but who approved one place, prospect, building, before another, so it does not appear that there ever was a man who would not have approved an action of humanity rather than of cruelty, interest and passion being quite out of the case. But interest and passion do come in, and are often too strong for and prevail over reflection and conscience. Now as brutes have various instincts by which they are carried on to the end the Author of their nature intended them for, is not man in the same condition, with this difference only that to his instincts (that is, appetites and passions) is added the principle of reflection or conscience? And as brutes act agreeably to their nature, in following that principle or particular instinct which for the present is strongest in them, does not man likewise act agreeably to his nature or obey the law of his creation by following that principle, be it passion or conscience, which for the present happens to be strongest in him? Thus different men are by their particular nature hurried on to pursue honor or riches or pleasure; there are also persons whose temper leads them in an uncommon degree to kindness, compassion, doing good to their fellow creatures, as there are others who are given to suspend their judgment, to weigh and consider things, and to act upon thought and reflection. Let everyone then quietly follow his nature, as passion, reflection, appetite, the several parts of it, happen to be strongest; but

let not the man of virtue take upon him to blame the ambitious, the covetous, the dissolute, since these equally with him obey and follow their nature. Thus, as in some cases we follow our nature in doing the works contained in the law, so in other cases we follow nature in doing contrary."

[4] Now all this licentious talk entirely goes upon a supposition that men follow their nature in the same sense, in violating the known rules of justice and honesty for the sake of a present gratification, as they do in following those rules when they have no temptation to the contrary. And if this were true, that could not be so which St. Paul asserts, that men are "by nature a law to themselves." If by following nature were meant only acting as we please, it would indeed be ridiculous to speak of nature as any guide in morals, nay, the very mention of deviating from nature would be absurd; and the mention of following it, when spoken by way of distinction, would absolutely have no meaning. For did ever any one act otherwise than as he pleased? And yet the ancients speak of deviating from nature as vice, and of following nature so much as a distinction, that according to them the perfection of virtue consists therein. So that language itself should teach people another sense of the words "following nature" than barely acting as we please. Let it however be observed that though the words "human nature" are to be explained, yet the real question of this discourse is not concerning the meaning of words—any other than as the explanation of them may be needful to make out and explain the assertion that every man is naturally a law to himself, that everyone may find within himself the rule of right, and obligations to follow it. This St. Paul affirms in the words of the text, and this the foregoing objection really denies by seeming to allow it. And the objection will be fully answered and the text before us explained, by observing that "nature" is considered in different views, and the words used in different senses; and by showing in what view it is considered, and in what sense the word is used, when intended to express and signify that which is the guide of life, that by which men are a law to themselves. I say the explanation of the term will be sufficient, because from thence it will appear that in some senses of the word "nature" cannot be, but that in another sense it manifestly is, a law to us.

[5] I. By nature is often meant no more than some principle in man, without regard either to the kind or degree of it. Thus the passion of anger and the affection of parents to their children would be called equally "natural." And as the same person hath often contrary principles, which at the same time draw contrary ways, he may by the same action both follow and contradict his nature in this sense of the word; he may follow one passion and contradict another.

[6] II. *Nature* is frequently spoken of as consisting in those passions which are strongest and most influence the actions; which being vicious ones, mankind is in this sense naturally vicious, or vicious by nature. Thus St. Paul says of the Gentiles, "who were dead in trespasses and sins, and walked according to the spirit of disobedience, that they were by nature

the children of wrath."[1] They could be no otherwise "children of wrath" by nature than they were vicious by nature.

[7] Here then are two different senses of the word "nature," in neither of which men can at all be said to be a law to themselves. They are mentioned only to be excluded, to prevent their being confounded, as the latter is in the objection, with another sense of it which is now to be inquired after and explained.

[8] III. The apostle asserts that the Gentiles "do by *nature* the things contained in the law." Nature is indeed here put by way of distinction from revelation, but yet it is not a mere negative. He intends to express more than that by which they *did not,* that by which they *did* the works of the law, namely, by *nature.* It is plain the meaning of the word is not the same in this passage as in the former, where it is spoken of as evil; for in this latter it is spoken of as good, as that by which they acted or might have acted virtuously. What that is in man by which he is "naturally a law to himself," is explained in the following words: "which show the work of the law written in their hearts, their conscience also bearing witness, and their thoughts the meanwhile accusing or else excusing one another."[2] If there be a distinction to be made between the *works written in their hearts* and the *witness of conscience,* by the former must be meant the natural disposition to kindness and compassion, to do what is of good report, to which this apostle often refers; that part of the nature of man, treated of in the foregoing discourse, which with very little reflection and of course leads him to society, and by means of which he naturally acts a just and good part in it unless other passions or interest lead him astray. Yet since other passions and regards to private interest, which lead us (though indirectly, yet they lead us) astray, are themselves in a degree equally natural and often most prevalent; and since we have no method of seeing the particular degrees in which one or the other is placed in us by nature, it is plain the former, considered merely as natural, good and right as they are, can no more be a law to us than the latter. But there is a superior principle of reflection or conscience in every man which distinguishes between the internal principles of his heart as well as his external actions, which passes judgment upon himself and them, pronounces determinately some actions to be in themselves just, right, good; others to be in themselves evil, wrong, unjust, which, without being consulted, without being advised with, magisterially exerts itself, and approves or condemns him the doer of them accordingly; and which, if not forcibly stopped, naturally and always of course goes on to anticipate a higher and more effectual sentence which shall hereafter second and affirm its own. But this part of the office of conscience is beyond my present design explicitly to consider. It is by this faculty, natural to man, that he is a moral agent, that he is a law to himself; by this faculty, I say, not to

1. *Ephes.* II: 3.

2. [*Rom.* II:15.]

be considered merely as a principle in his heart, which is to have some
influence as well as others, but considered as a faculty in kind and in
nature supreme over all others, and which bears its own authority of
being so.

[9] This *prerogative,* this *natural supremacy* of the faculty which sur-
veys, approves or disapproves, the several affections of our mind and
actions of our lives, being that by which men "are a law to themselves"—
their conformity or disobedience to which law of our nature renders their
actions, in the highest and most proper sense, natural or unnatural—it is
fit it be further explained to you, and I hope it will be so if you will attend
to the following reflections.

[10] Man may act according to that principle or inclination which
for the present happens to be strongest, and yet act in a way disproportionate to, and violate, his real proper nature. Suppose a brute creature
by any bait to be allured into a snare by which he is destroyed. He plainly
followed the bent of his nature, leading him to gratify his appetite; there
is an entire correspondence between his whole nature and such an action—
such action therefore is natural. But suppose a man, foreseeing the same
danger of certain ruin, should rush into it for the sake of a present gratification; he in this instance would follow his strongest desire, as did the
brute creature, but there would be as manifest a disproportion between the
nature of a man and such an action as between the meanest work of art
and the skill of the greatest master in that art; which disproportion arises,
not from considering the action singly in *itself* or in its *consequences,* but
from comparison of it with the nature of the agent. And since such an
action is utterly disproportionate to the nature of man, it is in the strictest
and most proper sense unnatural, this word expressing that disproportion.
Therefore, instead of the words "disproportionate to his nature," the
word "unnatural" may now be put, this being more familiar to us; but
let it be observed that it stands for the same thing precisely.

[11] Now what is it which renders such a rash action unnatural? Is it
that he went against the principle of reasonable and cool self-love considered *merely* as a part of his nature? No; for if he had acted the contrary way, he would equally have gone against a principle or part of his
nature, namely, passion or appetite. But to deny a present appetite, from
foresight that the gratification of it would end in immediate ruin or extreme misery, is by no means an unnatural action, whereas to contradict
or go against cool self-love for the sake of such gratification is so in the
instance before us. Such an action then being unnatural, and its being
so not arising from a man's going against a principle or desire barely, nor
in going against that principle or desire which happens for the present to
be strongest, it necessarily follows that there must be some other difference
or distinction to be made between these two principles, passion and cool
self-love, than what I have yet taken notice of. And this difference, not
being a difference in strength or degree, I call a difference in *nature* and
in *kind*. And since, in the instance still before us, if passion prevails over

self-love, the consequent action is unnatural; but if self-love prevails over
passion, the action is natural; it is manifest that self-love is in human nature a superior principle to passion. This may be contradicted without
violating that nature, but the former cannot. So that, if we will act conformably to the economy of man's nature, reasonable self-love must
govern. Thus, without particular consideration of conscience, we may
have a clear conception of the *superior nature* of one inward principle
to another, and see that there really is this natural superiority, quite distinct from degrees of strength and prevalency.

[12] Let us now take a view of the nature of man as consisting partly
of various appetites, passions, affections and partly of the principle of
reflection or conscience, leaving quite out all consideration of the different
degrees of strength in which either of them prevail, [and it will further appear that there is this natural superority of one inward principle to another, and that it is even part of the idea of reflection or conscience.][3]

[13] Passion or appetite implies a direct simple tendency toward such
and such objects, without distinction of the means by which they are to
be obtained. Consequently, it will often happen there will be a desire of
particular objects in cases where they cannot be obtained without manifest
injury to others. Reflection or conscience comes in, and disapproves the
pursuit of them in these circumstances; but the desire remains. Which
is to be obeyed, appetite or reflection? Cannot this question be answered,
from the economy and constitution of human nature merely, without saying which is strongest? Or need this at all come into consideration? Would
not the question be intelligibly and fully answered by saying that the
principle of reflection or conscience being compared with the various appetites, passions, and affections in men, the former is manifestly superior
and chief, without regard to strength? And how often soever the latter
happens to prevail, it is mere usurpation; the former remains in nature
and in kind its superior, and every instance of such prevalence of the latter is an instance of breaking in upon and violation of the constitution
of man.

[14] All this is no more than the distinction which everybody is acquainted with, between *mere power* and *authority;* only instead of being
intended to express the difference between what is possible and what is
lawful in civil government, here it has been shown applicable to the several
principles in the mind of man. Thus that principle by which we survey
and either approve or disapprove our own heart, temper, and actions, is
not only to be considered as what is in its turn to have some influence,
which may be said of every passion, of the lowest appetites, but likewise
as being superior; as from its very nature manifestly claiming superiority
over all others, insomuch that you cannot form a notion of this faculty,
conscience, without taking in judgment, direction, superintendency. This
is a constituent part of the idea, that is, of the faculty itself; and to preside

3. [This sentence was not in Ed. I.]

and govern, from the very economy and constitution of man, belongs to
it. Had it strength, as it his right; had it power, as it has manifest authority,
it would absolutely govern the world.

[15] This gives us a further view of the nature of man, shows us what
course of life we were made for; not only that our real nature leads us
to be influenced in some degree by reflection and conscience, but likewise in what degree we are to be influenced by it if we will fall in with and
act agreeably to the constitution of our nature; that this faculty was placed
within to be our proper governor, to direct and regulate all under principles, passions, and motives of action. This is its right and office; thus
sacred is its authority. And how often soever men violate and rebelliously
refuse to submit to it, for supposed interest which they cannot otherwise
obtain, or for the sake of passion which they cannot otherwise gratify,
this makes no alteration as to the *natural right* and *office* of conscience.

[16] Let us now turn this whole matter another way and suppose
there was no such thing at all as this natural supremacy of conscience, that
there was no distinction to be made between one inward principle and
another but only that of strength; and see what would be the consequence.

[17] Consider then what is the latitude and compass of the actions
of man with regard to himself, his fellow creatures, and the Supreme
Being? What are their bounds, besides that of our natural power? With
respect to the two first, they are plainly no other than these: no man seeks
misery as such for himself, and no one unprovoked does mischief to another for its own sake. For in every degree within these bounds, mankind
knowingly from passion or wantonness bring ruin and misery upon themselves and others. [And impiety and profaneness, I mean what everyone
would call so who believes the being of God, have absolutely no bounds
at all.][4] Men blaspheme the Author of nature, formally and in words
renounce their allegiance to their Creator. Put an instance then with
respect to any one of these three. [Though we should suppose profane
swearing, and in general that kind of impiety now mentioned, to mean
nothing, yet it implies wanton disregard and irreverence toward an infinite
Being, our Creator; and is this as suitable to the nature of man as reverence and dutiful submission of heart toward that Almighty Being? Or][5]
suppose a man guilty of parricide, with all the circumstances of cruelty
which such an action can admit of. This action is done in consequence of
its principle being for the present strongest; and if there be no difference
between inward principles but only that of strength, the strength being
given, you have the whole nature of the man given, so far as it relates
to this matter. The action plainly corresponds to the principle, the principle being in that degree of strength it was; it therefore corresponds to
the whole nature of the man. Upon comparing the action and the whole

4. [In Ed. I. this sentence ran thus: "And with respect to the Supreme Being there
is absolutely no bound at all to profaneness; I mean, that every one would call so
who believeth the Being of God."]

5. [This sentence was not in Ed. I.]

nature, there arises no disproportion, there appears no unsuitableness between them. Thus the murder of a father and the nature of man correspond to each other, as the same nature and an act of filial duty. If there be no difference between inward principles but only that of strength, we can make no distinction between these two actions, considered as the actions of such a creature; but in our coolest hours must approve or disapprove them equally; than which nothing can be reduced to a greater absurdity.

SERMON III

UPON HUMAN NATURE

For when the Gentiles, which have not the law, do by nature the things contained in the law, these, having not the law, are a law unto themselves (Romans II: 14).

[1] THE NATURAL SUPREMACY of reflection or conscience being thus established, we may from it form a distinct notion of what is meant by "human nature," when virtue is said to consist in following it, and vice in deviating from it.

[2] As the idea of a civil constitution implies in it united strength, various subordinations under one direction, that of the supreme authority, the different strength of each particular member of the society not coming into the idea; whereas, if you leave out the subordination, the union, and the one direction, you destroy and lose it; so reason, several appetites, passions, and affections, prevailing in different degrees of strength, is not *that* idea or notion of *human nature,* but *that nature* consists in these several principles considered as having a natural respect to each other, in the several passions being naturally subordinate to the one superior principle of reflection or conscience. Every bias, instinct, propension within is a real part of our nature, but not the whole; add to these the superior faculty, whose office it is to adjust, manage, and preside over them and take in this its natural superiority, and you complete the idea of human nature. And as in civil government the constitution is broken in upon and violated by power and strength prevailing over authority, so the constitution of man is broken in upon and violated by the lower faculties or principles within prevailing over that which is in its nature supreme over them all. Thus, when it is said by ancient writers that tortures and death are not so contrary to human nature as injustice—by this, to be sure, is not meant that the aversion to the former in mankind is less strong and prevalent than their aversion to the latter, but that the former is only

contrary to our nature considered in a partial view, and which takes in
only the lowest part of it, that which we have in common with the brutes;
whereas the latter is contrary to our nature considered, in a higher sense,
as a system and constitution contrary to the whole economy of man.[1]

[3] And from all these things put together, nothing can be more evident than that, exclusive of revelation, man cannot be considered as a
creature left by his Maker to act at random and live at large up to the
extent of his natural power, as passion, humor, wilfulness happen to
carry him, which is the condition brute creatures are in; but that from
his make, constitution, or nature, he is in the strictest and most proper
sense a law to himself. He hath the rule of right within; what is wanting is
only that he honestly attend to it.

[4] The inquiries which have been made by men of leisure, after some
general rule the conformity to, or disagreement from, which should denominate our actions good or evil, are in many respects of great service.
Yet let any plain honest man, before he engages in any course of action,
ask himself, Is this I am going about right, or is it wrong? Is it good, or
is it evil? I do not in the least doubt that this question would be answered
agreeably to truth and virtue, by almost any fair man in almost any circumstance. Neither do there appear any cases which look like exceptions to

---

1. Every man in his physical nature is one individual single agent. He has likewise
properties and principles, each of which may be considered separately and without
regard to the respects which they have to each other. Neither of these are the nature
we are taking a view of. But it is the inward frame of man considered as a *system* or
constitution—whose several parts are united, not by a physical principle of indi-
viduation, but by the respects they have to each other; the chief of which is the subjection which the appetites, passions, and particular affections have to the one
supreme principle of reflection or conscience. The system or constitution is formed
by and consists in these respects and this subjection. Thus the body is a *system* or
constitution; so is a tree; so is every machine. Consider all the several parts of a
tree without the natural respects they have to each other, and you have not at all
the idea of a tree; but add these respects, and this gives you the idea. The body may
be impaired by sickness, a tree may decay, a machine may be out of order, and yet
the system and constitution of them not totally dissolved. There is plainly somewhat
which answers to all this in the moral constitution of man. Whoever will consider
his own nature, will see that the several appetites, passions, and particular affections
have different respects amongst themselves. They are restraints upon, and are in a
proportion to, each other. [Cp. Serm. V, 13.] This proportion is just and perfect when
all those under principles are perfectly coincident with conscience, so far as their
nature permits, and in all cases under its absolute and entire direction. The least
excess or defect, the least alteration of the due proportions amongst themselves, or
of their coincidence with conscience, though not proceeding into action, is some
degree of disorder in the moral constitution. But perfection, though plainly intelligible and supposable, was never attained by any man. If the higher principle of
reflection maintains its place, and as much as it can corrects that disorder, and
hinders it from breaking out into action, this is all that can be expected in such a
creature as man. And though the appetites and passions have not their exact due
proportion to each other; though they often strive for mastery with judgment and
reflection; yet, since the superiority of this principle to all others is the chief respect
which forms the constitution, so far as this superiority is maintained, the character,
the man, is good, worthy, virtuous.

this, but those of superstition and of partiality to ourselves. Superstition may perhaps be somewhat of an exception; but partiality to ourselves is not, this being itself dishonesty. For a man to judge that to be the equitable, the moderate, the right part for him to act which he would see to be hard, unjust, oppressive in another—this is plain vice, and can proceed only from great unfairness of mind.

[5] But allowing that mankind hath the rule of right within himself, yet it may be asked, "What obligations are we under to attend to and follow it?" I answer, It has been proved that man by his nature is a law to himself, without the particular distinct consideration of the positive sanctions of that law; the rewards and punishments which we feel, and those which from the light of reason we have ground to believe are annexed to it. The question then carries its own answer along with it. Your obligation to obey this law is its being the law of your nature. That your conscience approves of and attests to such a course of action is itself alone an obligation. Conscience does not only offer itself to show us the way we should walk in, but it likewise carries its own authority with it; that it is our natural guide, the guide assigned us by the Author of our nature; it therefore belongs to our condition of being, it is our duty to walk in that path and follow this guide, without looking about to see whether we may not possibly forsake them with impunity.

[6] However, let us hear what is to be said against obeying this law of our nature. And the sum is no more than this: "Why should we be concerned about anything out of and beyond ourselves? If we do find within ourselves regards to others, and restraints of we know not how many different kinds, yet these being embarrassments and hindering us from going the nearest way to our own good, why should we not endeavor to suppress and get over them?"

[7] Thus people go on with words which, when applied to human nature and the condition in which it is placed in this world, have really no meaning. For does not all this kind of talk go upon supposition that our happiness in this world consists in somewhat quite distinct from regards to others, and that it is the privilege of vice to be without restraint or confinement? Whereas, on the contrary, the enjoyments, in a manner, all the common enjoyments of life, even the pleasures of vice, depend upon these regards of one kind or another to our fellow creatures. Throw off all regards to others, and we should be quite indifferent to infamy and to honor; there could be no such thing at all as ambition, and scarce any such thing as covetousness, for we should likewise be equally indifferent to the disgrace of poverty, the several neglects and kinds of contempt which accompany this state, and to the reputation of riches, the regard and respect they usually procure. Neither is restraint by any means peculiar to one course of life, but our very nature, exclusive of conscience and our condition, lays us under an absolute necessity of it. We cannot gain any end whatever without being confined to the proper means, which is often the most painful and uneasy confinement. And in numberless instances a present appetite cannot be gratified without such apparent and

immediate ruin and misery that the most dissolute man in the world chooses to forego the pleasure rather than endure the pain.

[8] Is the meaning then to indulge those regards to our fellow creatures, and submit to those restraints which upon the whole are attended with more satisfaction than uneasiness, and get over only those which bring more uneasiness and inconvenience than satisfaction? "Doubtless this was our meaning." You have changed sides then. Keep to this; be consistent with yourselves; and you and the men of virtue are *in general* perfectly agreed. But let us take care and avoid mistakes. Let it not be taken for granted that the temper of envy, rage, resentment yields greater delight than meekness, forgiveness, compassion, and goodwill; especially when it is acknowledged that rage, envy, resentment are in themselves mere misery; and the satisfaction arising from the indulgence of them is little more than relief from that misery, whereas the temper of compassion and benevolence is itself delightful; and the indulgence of it, by doing good, affords new positive delight and enjoyment. Let it not be taken for granted that the satisfaction arising from the reputation of riches and power, however obtained, and from the respect paid to them, is greater than the satisfaction arising from the reputation of justice, honesty, charity, and the esteem which is universally acknowledged to be their due. And if it be doubtful which of these satisfactions is the greatest, as there are persons who think neither of them very considerable, yet there can be no doubt concerning ambition and covetousness, virtue and a good mind, considered in themselves and as leading to different courses of life—there can, I say, be no doubt which temper and which course is attended with most peace and tranquility of mind, which with most perplexity, vexation, and inconvenience. And both the virtues and vices which have been now mentioned do in a manner equally imply in them regards of one kind or another to our fellow creatures. And with respect to restraint and confinement: whoever will consider the restraints from fear and shame, the dissimulation, mean arts of concealment, servile compliances—one or other of which belong to almost every course of vice—will soon be convinced that the man of virtue is by no means upon a disadvantage in this respect. How many instances are there in which men feel and own and cry aloud under the chains of vice with which they are enthralled, and which yet they will not shake off? How many instances in which persons manifestly go through more pains and self-denial to gratify a vicious passion than would have been necessary to the conquest of it? To this is to be added that when virtue is become habitual, when the temper of it is acquired, what was before "confinement" ceases to be so, by becoming choice and delight. Whatever restraint and guard upon ourselves may be needful to unlearn any unnatural distortion or odd gesture, yet, in all propriety of speech, natural behavior must be the most easy and unrestrained. It is manifest that, in the common course of life, there is seldom any inconsistency between our duty and what is *called* interest; it is much seldomer that there is any inconsistency between duty and what is really our present interest—meaning by "interest" happiness and satis-

faction. Self-love then, though confined to the interest of the present world, does in general perfectly coincide with virtue, and leads us to one and the same course of life. But, whatever exceptions there are to this, which are much fewer than they are commonly thought, all shall be set right at the final distribution of things. It is a manifest absurdity to suppose evil prevailing finally over good, under the conduct and administration of a perfect Mind.

[9] The whole argument which I have been now insisting upon, may be thus summed up and given you in one view: The Nature of man is adapted to some course of action or other. Upon comparing some actions with this nature, they appear suitable and correspondent to it; from comparison of other actions with the same nature, there arises to our view some unsuitableness or disproportion. The correspondence of actions to the nature of the agent renders them natural; their disproportion to it, unnatural. That an action is correspondent to the nature of the agent does not arise from its being agreeable to the principle which happens to be the strongest, for it may be so, and yet be quite disproportionate to the nature of the agent. The correspondence, therefore, or disproportion arises from somewhat else. This can be nothing but a difference in nature and kind, altogether distinct from strength, between the inward principles. Some then are in nature and kind superior to others. And the correspondence arises from the action being conformable to the higher principle, and the unsuitableness from its being contrary to it. Reasonable self-love and conscience are the chief or superior principles in the nature of man, because an action may be suitable to this nature, though all other principles be violated; but becomes unsuitable, if either of those are. Conscience and self-love, if we understand our true happiness, always lead us the same way. Duty and interest are perfectly coincident, for the most part in this world, but entirely and in every instance if we take in the future and the whole, this being implied in the notion of a good and perfect administration of things. Thus they who have been so wise in their generation as to regard only their own supposed interest, at the expense and to the injury of others, shall at last find that he who has given up all the advantages of the present world rather than violate his conscience and the relations of life, has infinitely better provided for himself and secured his own interest and happiness.

SERMON IV*

UPON THE LOVE OF OUR NEIGHBOR[1]

And if there be any other commandment, it is briefly comprehended in this saying, namely, Thou shalt love thy neighbour as thyself (Romans XIII: 9).

[1] IT IS COMMONLY OBSERVED that there is a disposition in men to complain of the viciousness and corruption of the age in which they live, as greater than that of former ones; which is usually followed with this further observation that mankind has been in that respect much the same in all times. Now, not to determine whether this last be not contradicted by the accounts of history, thus much can scarce be doubted—that vice and folly takes different turns, and some particular kinds of it are more open and avowed in some ages than in others; and I suppose it may be spoken of as very much the distinction of the present to profess a contracted spirit and greater regards to self-interest than appears to have been done formerly. Upon this account it seems worth while to inquire whether private interest is likely to be promoted in proportion to the degree in which self-love engrosses us, and prevails over all other principles, or whether the contracted affection may not possibly be so prevalent as to disappoint itself, and even contradict its own end, private good.

[2] And since, further, there is generally thought to be some peculiar kind of contrariety between self-love and the love of our neighbor, between the pursuit of public and of private good, insomuch that when you are recommending one of these, you are supposed to be speaking against the other; and from hence arises a secret prejudice against and frequently open scorn of all talk of public spirit and real goodwill to our fellow creatures; it will be necessary to inquire what respect benevolence hath to self-love, and the pursuit of private interest to the pursuit of public; or whether there be anything of that peculiar inconsistency and contrariety between them, over and above what there is between self-love and other passions and particular affections, and their respective pursuits.

[3] These inquiries, it is hoped, may be favorably attended to; for there shall be all possible concessions made to the favorite passion, which hath so much allowed to it, and whose cause is so universally pleaded: it shall be treated with the utmost tenderness and concern for its interests.

[4] In order to this, as well as to determine the forementioned questions, it will be necessary to consider the nature, the object, and end of that self-love, as distinguished from other principles or affections in the mind and their respective objects.

*[Sermon XI of the complete edition—Ed.]

1. Preached on Advent Sunday.

[5] Every man hath a generál desire of his own happiness, and like-wise a variety of particular affections, passions, and appetites to particular external objects. The former proceeds from or is self-love, and seems inseparable from all sensible creatures who can reflect upon themselves and their own interest or happiness, so as to have that interest an object to their minds; what is to be said of the latter is that they proceed from, or together make up, that particular nature according to which man is made. The object the former pursues is somewhat internal—our own happiness, enjoyment, satisfaction; whether we have or have not a dis-tinct particular perception what it is or wherein it consists, the objects of the latter are this or that particular external thing which the affections tend towards, and of which it hath always a particular idea or perception. The principle we call "self-love" never seeks anything external for the sake of the thing, but only as a means of happiness or good; particular affections rest in the external things themselves. One belongs to man as a reasonable creature [reflecting upon his own interest or happiness].[2] The other, though quite distinct from reason, are as much a part of human nature.

[6] That all particular appetites and passions are toward *external things themselves,* distinct from the *pleasure arising from them,* is mani-fested from hence—that there could not be this pleasure were it not for that prior suitableness between the object and the passion; there could be no enjoyment or delight from one thing more than another, from eating food more than from swallowing a stone, if there were not an affec-tion or appetite to one thing more than another.

[7] Every particular affection, even the love of our neighbor, is as really our own affection as self-love; and the pleasure arising from its gratification is as much my own pleasure as the pleasure self-love would have from knowing I myself should be happy some time hence, would be my own pleasure. And if, because every particular affection is a man's own, and the pleasure arising from its gratification his own pleasure, or pleasure to himself, such particular affection must be called self-love, ac-cording to this way of speaking no creature whatever can possibly act but merely from self-love; and every action and every affection whatever is to be resolved up into this one principle. But then this is not the lan-guage of mankind; or if it were, we should want words to express the difference between the principle of an action proceeding from cool con-sideration that it will be to my own advantage, and an action, suppose of revenge or of friendship, by which a man runs upon certain ruin to do evil or good to another. It is manifest the principles of these actions are totally different, and so want different words to be distinguished by; all that they agree in is that they both proceed from and are done to gratify an inclination in a man's self. But the principle or inclination in one case is self-love, in the other, hatred or love of another. There is then a dis-tinction between the cool principle of self-love or general desire of our

2. [Not in Ed. I.]

happiness, as one part of our nature and one principle of action, and the
particular affections toward particular external objects, as another part
of our nature and another principle of action. How much soever therefore
is to be allowed to self-love, yet it cannot be allowed to be the whole of
our inward constitution, because, you see, there are other parts or principles which come into it.

[8] Further, private happiness or good is all which self-love can make
us desire or be concerned about; in having this consists its gratification:
it is an affection to ourselves, a regard to our own interest, happiness, and
private good; and in the proportion a man hath this, he is interested, or a
lover of himself. Let this be kept in mind; because there is commonly, as I
shall presently have occasion to observe, another sense put upon these
words. On the other hand, particular affections tend toward particular
external things; these are their objects; having these is their end—in this
consists their gratification, no matter whether it be, or be not, upon the
whole, our interest or happiness. An action done from the former of these
principles is called an interested action. An action proceeding from any
of the latter has its denomination of passionate, ambitious, friendly, re-
vengeful, or any other, from the particular appetite or affection from
which it proceeds. Thus self-love as one part of human nature and the
several particular principles as the other part are, themselves, their objects
and ends, stated and shown.

[9] From hence it will be easy to see how far, and in what ways, each
of these can contribute and be subservient to the private good of the
individual. Happiness does not consist in self-love. The desire of happiness is no more the thing itself than the desire of riches is the possession
or enjoyment of them. People may love themselves with the most entire
and unbounded affection, and yet be extremely miserable. Neither can
self-love anyway help them out, but by setting them on work to get rid
of the causes of their misery, to gain or make use of those objects which
are by nature adapted to afford satisfaction. Happiness or satisfaction consists only in the enjoyment of those objects which are by nature suited
to our several particular appetites, passions, and affections. So that if
self-love wholly engrosses us, and leaves no room for any other principle,
there can be absolutely no such thing at all as happiness, or enjoyment
of any kind whatever, since happiness consists in the gratification of particular passions, which supposes the having of them. Self-love then does
not constitute *this* or *that* to be our interest or good; but, our interest or
good being constituted by nature and supposed, self-love only puts us
upon obtaining and securing it. Therefore, if it be possible that self-love
may prevail and exert itself in a degree or manner which is not subservient
to this end, then it will not follow that our interest will be promoted in
proportion to the degree in which that principle engrosses us, and prevails
over others. Nay further, the private and contracted affection, when it is
not subservient to this end, private good, may, for anything that appears,
have a direct contrary tendency and effect. And if we will consider the
matter, we shall see that it often really has. *Disengagement* is absolutely

necessary to enjoyment; and a person may have so steady and fixed an eye upon his own interest, whatever he places it in, as may hinder him from *attending* to many gratifications within his reach, which others have their minds free and open to. Overfondness for a child is not generally thought to be for its advantage; and if there be any guess to be made from appearances, surely that character we call selfish is not the most promising for happiness. Such a temper may plainly be, and exert itself [in a degree and manner which may give unnecessary and useless solicitude and anxiety,][3] in a degree and manner which may prevent obtaining the means and materials of enjoyment, as well as the making use of them. Immoderate self-love does very ill consult its own interest; and how much soever a paradox it may appear, it is certainly true that even from self-love we should endeavor to get over all inordinate regard to and consideration of ourselves. [Every one of our passions and affections hath its natural stint and bound, which may easily be exceeded; whereas our enjoyments can possibly be but in a determinate measure and degree. Therefore such excess of the affection, since it cannot procure any enjoyment, must in all cases be useless, but is generally attended with inconveniences, and often is downright pain and misery. This holds as much with regard to self-love as to all other affections. The natural degree of it,][4] so far as it sets us on work to gain and make use of the materials of satisfaction, may be to our real advantage; but beyond or besides this, it is in several respects an inconvenience and disadvantage. Thus it appears that private interest is so far from being likely to be promoted in proportion to the degree in which self-love engrosses us, and prevails over all other principles, that the contracted affection may be so prevalent as to disappoint itself, and even contradict its own end, private good.

[10] "But who, except the most sordidly covetous, ever thought there was any rivalship between the love of greatness, honor, power, or between sensual appetites and self-love? No, there is a perfect harmony between them. It is by means of these particular appetites and affections that self-love is gratified in enjoyment, happiness, and satisfaction. The competition and rivalship is between self-love and the love of our neighbor, that affection which leads us out of ourselves, makes us regardless of our own interest, and substitute that of another in its stead." Whether then there be any peculiar competition and contrariety in this case, shall now be considered.

[11] Self-love and interestedness was stated to consist in or be an affection to ourselves, a regard to our own private good; it is therefore distinct from benevolence, which is an affection to the good of our fellow creatures. But that benevolence is distinct from, that is, not the same thing with self-love, is no reason for its being looked upon with any pe-

---

3. [Not in Ed. I.]

4. [In Ed. I., this passage was shorter, and ran as follows: "Every one of our faculties has its stint and bound: our enjoyments can be but in a determinate measure and degree. The principle of self-love, so far as it sets us on work," etc.]

culiar suspicion; because every principle whatever, by means of which self-love is gratified, is distinct from it; and all things which are distinct from each other are equally so. A man has an affection or aversion to another; that one of these tends to and is gratified by doing good, that the other tends to and is gratified by doing harm, does not in the least alter the respect which either one or the other of these inward feelings has to self-love. We use the word "property" so as to exclude any other persons having an interest in that of which we say a particular man has the property. And we often use the word "selfish" so as to exclude in the same manner all regards to the good of others. [But the cases are not parallel; for though that exclusion is really part of the idea of property, yet such positive exclusion, or bringing this peculiar disregard to the good of others into the idea of self-love, is in reality adding to the idea, or changing it from what it was before stated to consist in, namely, in an affection to ourselves.[5] This being the whole idea of self-love, it can no otherwise exclude goodwill or love of others than merely by not including it, no otherwise than it excludes love of arts or reputation, or of anything else. Neither, on the other hand, does benevolence, any more than love of arts or of reputation, exclude self-love. Love of our neighbor then][6] has just the same respect to, is no more distant from, self-love than hatred of our neighbor, or than love or hatred of anything else. Thus the principles from which men rush upon certain ruin for the destruction of an enemy, and for the preservation of a friend, have the same respect to the private affection, and are equally interested or equally disinterested; and it is of no avail whether they are said to be one or the other. Therefore, to those that are shocked[7] to hear virtue spoken of as disinterested, it may be allowed that it is indeed absurd to speak thus of it, unless hatred, several particular instances of vice, and all the common affections and aversions in mankind are acknowledged to be disinterested too. Is there any less inconsistency between the love of inanimate things, or of creatures merely sensitive, and self-love than between self-love and the love of our neighbor? Is desire of and delight in the happiness of another any more a diminution of self-love than desire of and delight in the esteem of another?

5. § 8.

6. [In Ed. I., these sentences run as follows: "And as it is taken for granted in the former case, that the external good, in which we have a property exclusive of all others, must for this reason have a nearer and greater respect to private interest than it would have if it were enjoyed in common with others; so likewise it is taken for granted that the principle of an action which does not proceed from regard to the good of others has a nearer and greater respect to self-love, or is less distant from it. But whoever will at all attend to the thing, will see that these consequences do not follow. For as the enjoyment of the air we breathe is just as much our private interest and advantage now as it would be if none but ourselves had the benefit of it, so love of our neighbor," etc.]

7. [It should be remembered that, in the language of Butler's day, "shocked" means nothing more than "surprised," and does not connote *painful* surprise.]

They are both equally desire of and delight in somewhat external to ourselves: either both or neither are so. The object of self-love is expressed in the term "self"; and every appetite of sense and every particular affection of the heart are equally interested or disinterested, because the objects of them are all equally self or somewhat else. Whatever ridicule therefore the mention of a disinterested principle or action may be supposed to lie open to, must, upon the matter being thus stated, relate to ambition and every appetite and particular affection, as much as to benevolence. And indeed all the ridicule and all the grave perplexity, of which this subject hath had its full share, is merely from words. The most intelligible way of speaking of it seems to be this: that self-love and the actions done in consequence of it (for these will presently appear to be the same as to this question) are interested; that particular affections toward external objects, and the actions done in consequence of those affections, are not so. But everyone is at liberty to use words as he pleases. All that is here insisted upon is that amibition, revenge, benevolence, all particular passions whatever, and the actions they produce, are equally interested or disinterested.

[12] [Thus it appears that there is no peculiar contrariety between self-love and benevolence, no greater competition between these than between any other particular affections and self-love. This relates to the affections themselves. Let us now see whether there be any peculiar contrariety between the respective courses of life which these affections lead to, whether there be any greater competition between the pursuit of private and of public good than between any other particular pursuits and that of private good.

[13] There seems no other reason to suspect that there is any such peculiar contrariety, but only that the course of action which benevolence leads to has a more direct tendency to promote the good of others than that course of action which love of reputation suppose, or any other particular affection leads to. But that any affection tends to the happiness of another does not hinder its tending to one's own happiness too. That others enjoy the benefit of the air and the light of the sun does not hinder but that these are as much one's own private advantage now as they would be if we had the property of them exclusive of all others. So a pursuit which tends to promote the good of another, yet may have as great tendency to promote private interest as a pursuit which does not tend to the good of another at all or which is mischievous to him. All particular affections whatever, resentment, benevolence, love of arts, equally lead to a course of action for their own gratification, that is, the gratification of ourselves; and the gratification of each gives delight; so far then it is manifest they have all the same respect to private interest. Now take into consideration further, concerning these three pursuits, that the end of the first is the harm, of the second, the good of another, of the last, somewhat indifferent; and is there any necessity that these additional considerations should alter the respect which we before saw these three pursuits had to private interest, or render any one of them less conducive

to it than any other?][8] Thus one man's affection is to honor as his end, in order to obtain which he thinks no pains too great. Suppose another, with such a singularity of mind as to have the same affection to public good as his end, which he endeavors with the same labor to obtain. In case of success, surely the man of benevolence hath as great enjoyment as the man of ambition; they both equally having the end their affections, in the same degree, tended to; but in case of disappointment, the benevolent man has clearly the advantage, since endeavoring to do good, considered as a virtuous pursuit, is gratified by its own consciousness, that is, is in a degree its own reward.

[14] And as to these two, or [benevolence and][9] any other particular passions whatever, considered in a further view as forming a general temper which more or less disposes us for enjoyment of all the common blessings of life, distinct from their own gratification, is benevolence less the temper of tranquility and freedom than ambition or covetousness? Does the benevolent man appear less easy with himself, from his love to his neighbor? Does he less relish his being? Is there any peculiar gloom seated on his face? Is his mind less open to entertainment, to any particular gratification? Nothing is more manifest than that being in good humor, which is benevolence whilst it lasts, is itself the temper of satisfaction and enjoyment.

[15] Suppose then a man sitting down to consider how he might become most easy to himself and attain the greatest pleasure he could—all that which is his real natural happiness. This can only consist in the enjoyment of those objects which are by nature adapted to our several faculties. These particular enjoyments make up the sum total of our happiness; and they are supposed to arise from riches, honors, and the gratification of sensual appetites; be it so, yet none profess themselves so completely happy in these enjoyments but that there is room left in the mind for others if they were presented to them; nay, these, as much as they engage us, are not thought so high but that human nature is capable even of greater. Now there have been persons in all ages who have professed that they found satisfaction in the exercise of charity, in the love of their neighbor, in endeavoring to promote the happiness of all they had to do with, and in the pursuit of what is just and right and good, as the general bent of their mind and end of their life; and that doing an action of baseness or cruelty would be as great violence to *their* self as much breaking in upon their nature as any external force. Persons of this character would add, if they might be heard, that they consider themselves as acting in the

8. [§ 12 and § 13 down to the words "any other" were not in Ed. I., which had instead: "But since self-love is not private good, since interestedness is not interest, let us now see whether benevolence has not the same respect to, the same tendency toward promoting, private good and interest, with the other particular passions; as it hath been already shown that they have all in common the same respect to self-love and interestedness. One man's," etc.]

9. [Not in Ed. I.]

view of an infinite Being, who is in a much higher sense the object of reverence and of love than all the world besides; and therefore they could have no more enjoyment from a wicked action committed under His eye than the persons to whom they are making their apology could, if all mankind were the spectators of it; and that the satisfaction of approving themselves to His unerring judgment, to Whom they thus refer all their actions, is a more continued settled satisfaction than any this world can afford; [as also that they have, no less than others, a mind free and open to all the common innocent gratifications of it, such as they are.][10] And if we go no further, does there appear any absurdity in this? Will any one take it upon him to say that a man cannot find his account in this general course of life as much as in the most unbounded ambition and the excesses of pleasure? Or that such a person has not consulted so well for himself, for the satisfaction and peace of his own mind, as the ambitious or dissolute man? And though the consideration that God Himself will in the end justify their taste, and support their cause, is not formally to be insisted upon here, yet thus much comes in, that all enjoyments whatever are much more clear and unmixed from the assurance that they will end well. Is it certain then that there is nothing in these pretensions to happiness, especially when there are not wanting persons who have supported themselves with satisfactions of this kind in sickness, poverty, disgrace, and in the very pangs of death, whereas it is manifest all other enjoyments fail in these circumstances? This surely looks suspicious of having somewhat in it. Self-love methinks should be alarmed. May she not possibly pass over greater pleasures than those she is so wholly taken up with?

[16] The short of the matter is no more than this: happiness consists in the gratification of certain affections, appetites, passions, with objects which are by nature adapted to them. Self-love may indeed set us on work to gratify these, but happiness or enjoyment has no immediate connection with self-love, but arises from such gratification alone. Love of our neighbor is one of those affections. This, considered as a *virtuous principle,* is gratified by a consciousness of endeavoring to promote the good of others; but considered as a *natural affection,* its gratification consists in the actual accomplishment of this endeavor. Now indulgence [or gratification][11] of this affection, whether in that consciousness or this accomplishment, has the same respect to interest as indulgence of any other affection; they equally proceed from or do not proceed from self-love; they equally include or equally exclude this principle. Thus it appears that benevolence and the pursuit of public good hath at least as great respect to self-love and the pursuit of private good as any other particular passions, and their respective pursuits.

[17] Neither is covetousness, whether as a temper or pursuit, any exception to this. For if by covetousness is meant the desire and pursuit of

10. [Not in Ed. I.]

11. [Not in Ed. I.]

riches for their own sake, without any regard to, or consideration of, the uses of them, this hath as little to do with self-love as benevolence hath. But by this word is usually meant, not such madness and total distraction of mind, but immoderate affection to and pursuit of riches as possessions in order to some further end, namely, satisfaction, interest, or good. This therefore is not a particular affection or particular pursuit, but it is the general principle of self-love and the general pursuit of our own interest; for which reason the word "selfish" is by everyone appropriated to this temper and pursuit. Now, as it is ridiculous to assert that self-love and the love of our neighbor are the same, so neither is it asserted that following these different affections hath the same tendency and respect to our own interest. The comparison is not between self-love and the love of our neighbor, between pursuit of our own interest and the interest of others, but between the several particular affections in human nature toward external objects, as one part of the comparison, and the one particular affection to the good of our neighbor, as the other part of it; and it has been shown that all these have the same respect to self-love and private interest.

[18] There is indeed frequently an inconsistency or interfering between self-love or private interest and the several particular appetites, passions, affections, or the pursuits they lead to. But this competition or interfering is merely accidental, and happens much oftener between pride, revenge, sensual gratifications, and private interest than between private interest and benevolence. For nothing is more common than to see men give themselves up to a passion or an affection to their known prejudice and ruin, and in direct contradiction to manifest and real interest and the loudest calls of self-love; whereas the seeming competitions and interfering between benevolence and private interest relate much more to the materials or means of enjoyment than to enjoyment itself. There is often an interfering in the former, when there is none in the latter. Thus as to riches: so much money as a man gives away, so much less will remain in his possession. Here is a real interfering. But though a man cannot possibly give without lessening his fortune, yet there are multitudes might give without lessening their own enjoyment, because they may have more than they can turn to any real use or advantage to themselves. Thus, the more thought and time anyone employs about the interests and good of others, he must necessarily have less to attend his own; but he may have so ready and large a supply of his own wants that such thought might be really useless to himself, though of great service and assistance to others.

[19] The general mistake,[12] that there is some greater inconsistency between endeavoring to promote the good of another and self-interest than between self-interest and pursuing anything else, [seems, as hath already been hinted, to arise from our notions of property; and to be carried on by this property's being supposed to be itself our happiness or good. People are so very much taken up with this one subject that they

12. [Ed. I. has "The occasion of the general mistake," etc.]

seem from it to have formed a general way of thinking, which they apply to other things that they have nothing to do with. Hence, in a confused and slight way, it might well be taken for granted that another's having no interest in an affection (that is, his good not being the object of it), renders, as one may speak, the proprietor's interest in it greater; and that if another had an interest in it, this would render his less, or occasion that such affection could not be so friendly to self-love, or conducive to private good, as an affection or pursuit which has not a regard to the good of another. This, I say, might be taken for granted, whilst it was not attended to that the object of every particular affection is equally somewhat external to ourselves; and whether it be the good of another person, or whether it be any other external thing, makes no alteration with regard to its being one's own affection, and the gratification of it one's own private enjoyment. And so far as it is taken for granted that barely having the means and materials of enjoyment is what constitutes interest and happiness; that our interest or good consists in possessions themselves, in having the property of riches, houses, lands, gardens, not in the enjoyment of them; so far it will even more strongly be taken for granted, in the way already explained, that an affection's conducing to the good of another must even necessarily occasion it to conduce less to private good, if not to be positively detrimental to it. For if property and happiness are one and the same thing, as by increasing the property of another, you lessen your own property, so by promoting the happiness of another, you must lessen your own happiness.][13] But whatever occasioned the mistake, I hope it has been fully proved to be one, [as it has been proved that there is no peculiar rivalship or competition between self-love and benevolence; that as there may be a competition between these two, so there may also between any particular affection whatever and self-love; that every particular affection, benevolence among the rest, is subservient to self-love by being the instrument of private enjoyment; and that in one respect benevolence contributes more to private interest, that is, enjoyment or satisfaction, than any other of the particular common affections, as it is in a degree of its own gratification.][14]

[20] And to all these things may be added that religion, [from whence arises our strongest obligation to benevolence,][15] is so far from disowning

13. [This was all expressed differently in Ed. I., which, after the words "anything else" in line 4 of the section, proceeded: "is this which hath been already hinted, that men consider the means and materials of enjoyment, not the enjoyment of them, as what constitutes interest and happiness. It is the possession, having the property of riches, houses, lands, gardens, in which our interest or good is supposed to consist. Now, if riches and happiness are identical terms, it may well be thought that, as by bestowing riches on another, you lessen your own, so also by promoting the happiness of another you lessen your own. And thus there would be a real inconsistence and contrariety between private and public good."]

14. [Not in Ed. I.]

15. [Not in Ed. I.]

the principle of self-love that it often addresses itself to that very principle, and always to the mind in that state when reason presides; and there can no access be had to the understanding but by convincing men that the course of life we would persuade them to is not contrary to their interest. It may be allowed, without any prejudice to the cause of virtue and religion, that our ideas of happiness and misery are of all our ideas the nearest and most important to us, that they will, nay, if you please, that they ought to prevail over those of order and beauty and harmony and proportion if there should ever be, as it is impossible there ever should be, any inconsistency between them, though these last, too, as expressing the fitness of actions, are real as truth itself. Let it be allowed, though virtue or moral rectitude does indeed consist in affection to and pursuit of what is right and good, as such, yet, that when we sit down in a cool hour, we can neither justify to ourselves this or any other pursuit till we are convinced that it will be for our happiness or at least not contrary to it.

[21] Common reason and humanity will have some influence upon mankind, whatever becomes of speculations; but, so far as the interests of virtue depend upon the theory of it being secured from open scorn, so far its very being in the world depends upon its appearing to have no contrariety to private interest and self-love. The foregoing observations, therefore, it is hoped, may have gained a little ground in favor of the precept before us; the particular explanation of which shall be the subject of the next discourse.

[22] I will conclude at present with observing the peculiar obligation which we are under to virtue and religion, as enforced in the verses following the text, in the Epistle for the day, from our Saviour's coming into the world. "The night is far spent, the day is at hand; let us therefore cast off the works of darkness, and let us put on the armour of light," etc.[16] The meaning and force of which exhortation is that Christianity lays us under new obligations to a good life, as by it the will of God is more clearly revealed, and as it affords additional motives to the practice of it, over and above those which arise out of the nature of virtue and vice; I might add, As our Saviour has set us a perfect example of goodness in our own nature. Now love and charity is plainly the thing in which He hath placed His religion; in which therefore, as we have any pretense to the name of Christians, we must place ours. He hath at once enjoined it upon us by way of command with peculiar force and by His example, as having undertaken the work of our salvation out of pure love and goodwill to mankind. The endeavor to set home this example upon our minds is a very proper employment of this season, which is bringing on the festival of His Birth; which as it may teach us many excellent lessons of humility, resignation, and obedience to the will of God, so there is none it recommends with greater authority, force and advantage than this of love and charity; since it was "for us men and for our salvation" that "He came down from heaven, and was incarnate, and was made

16. [*Rom.* XIII: 12.]

man"; that He might teach us our duty, and more especially that He might enforce the practice of it, reform mankind, and finally bring us to that "eternal salvation," of which "He is the Author to all those that obey Him."[17]

17. [*Heb.* V: 9.]

SERMON V*

UPON THE LOVE OF OUR NEIGHBOR

And if there be any other commandment, it is briefly comprehended in this saying, namely, Thou shalt love thy neighbour as thyself (Romans XIII: 9).

[1] HAVING ALREADY REMOVED the prejudices against public spirit, or the love of our neighbor, on the side of private interest and self-love, I proceed to the particular explanation of the precept before us, by showing: who is our neighbor; in what sense we are required to love him as ourselves; the influence such love would have upon our behavior in life; and lastly, how this commandment comprehends in it all others.

[2] I. The objects and due extent of this affection will be understood by attending to the nature of it, and to the nature and circumstances of mankind in this world. The love of our neighbor is the same with charity, benevolence, or goodwill: it is an affection to the good and happiness of our fellow creatures. This implies in it a disposition to produce happiness; and this is the simple notion of goodness, which appears so amiable wherever we meet with it. From hence it is easy to see that the perfection of goodness consists in love to the whole universe. [This is the perfection of Almighty God][1].

[3] But as man is so much limited in his capacity, as so small a part of the creation comes under his notice and influence, and as we are not used to consider things in so general a way, it is not to be thought of, that the universe should be the object of benevolence to such creatures as we are.

*[Sermon XII of the complete edition—Ed.]

1. [For this Ed. I. had: "Thus we are commanded to be 'perfect as our Father which is in heaven is perfect' (*St. Matt.* V: 48), *i.e.* perfect in goodness or benevolence as the preceding words determine the sense to be; to make the object of this affection as general and extensive as we are able."]

[Thus in that precept of our Saviour, "Be ye perfect, even as your Father, which is in heaven, is perfect,"[2] the perfection of the Divine goodness is proposed to our imitation as it is promiscuous and extends to the evil as well as the good; not as it is absolutely universal, imitation of it in this respect being plainly beyond us. The object is too vast. For this reason][3] moral writers also have substituted a less general object for our benevolence, mankind. But this likewise is an object too general, and very much out of our view. Therefore persons more practical have, instead of mankind, put our country, and made the principle of virtue, of human virtue, to consist in the entire uniform love of our country; and this is what we call a public spirit; which in men of public stations is the character of a patriot. But this is speaking to the upper part of the world. Kingdoms and governments are large; and the sphere of action of far the greatest part of mankind is much narrower than the government they live under; or however, common men do not consider their actions as affecting the whole community of which they are members. There plainly is wanting a less general and nearer object of benevolence for the bulk of men than that of their country. Therefore the Scripture, not being a book of theory and speculation, but a plain rule of life for mankind, has with the utmost possible propriety put the principle of virtue upon the love of our neighbor; which is that part of the universe, that part of mankind, that part of our country, which comes under our immediate notice, acquaintance, and influence, and with which we have to do.

[4] This is plainly the true account or reason why our Saviour places the principle of virtue in the love of our *neighbor;* and the account itself shows who are comprehended under that relation.

[5] II. Let us now consider in what sense we are commanded to love our neighbor *as ourselves.*

[6] This precept, in its first delivery by our Saviour is thus introduced: "Thou shalt love the Lord thy God with all thine heart, with all thy soul, and with all thy strength; and thy neighbor as thyself."[4] These very different manners of expression do not lead our thoughts to the same measure or degree of love, common to both objects, but to one, peculiar to each. Supposing then, which is to be supposed, a distinct meaning and propriety in the words, "as thyself"; the precept we are considering will admit of any of these senses: that we bear the *same kind* of affection to our neighbor as we do to ourselves; or, that the love we bear to our neighbor should have *some certain proportion or other* to self-love; or, lastly, that it should bear the particular proportion of *equality,* that *it be in the same degree.*

[7] First, the precept may be understood as requiring only that we have the *same kind* of affection to our fellow creatures as to ourselves: that, as

2. *St. Matt.* V: 48.

3. [These sentences were not in Ed. I. at this point.]

4. [*St. Matt.* XXII: 37.]

every man has the principle of self-love, which disposes him to avoid misery and consult his own happiness, so we should cultivate the affection of goodwill to our neighbor, and that it should influence us to have the same kind of regard to him. This at least must be commanded; and this will not only prevent our being injurious to him, but will also put us upon promoting his good. There are blessings in life which we share in common with others: peace, plenty, freedom, healthful seasons. But real benevolence to our fellow creatures would give us the notion of a common interest in a stricter sense; for in the degree we love another, his interest, his joys and sorrows, are our own. It is from self-love that we form the notion of private good and consider it as our own; love of our neighbor would teach us thus to appropriate to ourselves his good and welfare, to consider ourselves as having a real share in his happiness. Thus the principle of benevolence would be an advocate within our own breasts, to take care of the interests of our fellow creatures in all the interfering and competitions which cannot but be, from the imperfection of our nature, and the state we are in. It would likewise, in some measure, lessen that interfering, and hinder men from forming so strong a notion of private good, exclusive of the good of others, as we commonly do. Thus, as the private affection makes us in a peculiar manner sensible of humanity, justice or injustice, when exercised toward ourselves, love of our neighbor would give us the same kind of sensibility in his behalf. This would be the greatest security of our uniform obedience to that most equitable rule: "Whatsoever ye would that men should do to you, do ye even so to them."[5]

[8] All this is indeed no more than that we should have a real love to our neighbor; but then, which is to be observed, the words "as thyself" express this in the most distinct manner, and determine the precept to relate to the affection itself. The advantage which this principle of benevolence has over other remote considerations is that it is itself the temper of virtue; and likewise, that it is the chief, nay, the only effectual security of our performing the several offices of kindness we owe to our fellow creatures. When from distant considerations men resolve upon anything to which they have no liking, or perhaps an averseness, they are perpetually finding out evasions and excuses, which need never be wanting if people look for them; and they equivocate with themselves in the plainest cases in the world. This may be in respect to single determinate acts of virtue; but it comes in much more where the obligation is to a general course of behavior, and most of all if it be such as cannot be reduced to fixed determinate rules. This observation may account for the diversity of the expression, in that known passage of the prophet Micah: "to do justly, and to love mercy."[6] A man's heart must be formed to humanity and benevolence, he must *love mercy,* otherwise he will not act mercifully in any settled course of behavior. As consideration of the future sanctions

5. [*St. Matt.* VII: 12.]

6. [*Micah* VI: 8.]

of religion is our only security of persevering in our duty, in cases of great temptation, so to get our heart and temper formed to a love and liking of what is good, is absolutely necessary in order to our behaving rightly in the familiar and daily intercourses amongst mankind.

[9] Secondly, the precept before us may be understood to require that we love our neighbor in some certain *proportion* or other *according as* we love ourselves. And indeed a man's character cannot be determined by the love he bears to his neighbor, considered absolutely; but the proportion which this bears to self-love, whether it be attended to or not, is the chief thing which forms the character and influences the actions. For as the form of the body is a composition of various parts, so likewise our inward structure is not simple or uniform, but a composition of various passions, appetites, affections, together with rationality, including in this last both the discernment of what is right and a disposition to regulate ourselves by it. There is greater variety of parts in what we call a character than there are features in a face; and the morality of that is no more determined by one part than the beauty or deformity of this is by one single feature; each is to be judged of by all the parts or features, not taken singly but together. In the inward frame the various passions, appetites, affections stand in different respects to each other. The principles in our mind may be contradictory, or checks and allays only, or incentives and assistants to each other. And principles which in their nature have no kind of contrarariety of affinity may yet accidentally be each other's allays or incentives.

[10] From hence it comes to pass that though we were able to look into the inward contexture of the heart, and see with the greatest exactness in what degree any one principle is in a particular man, we could not from thence determine how far that principle would go toward forming the character, or what influence it would have upon the actions, unless we could likewise discern what other principles prevailed in him, and see the proportion which that one bears to the others. Thus, though two men should have the affection of compassion in the same degree exactly, yet one may have the principle of resentment, or of ambition, so strong in him as to prevail over that of compassion and prevent its having any influence upon his actions, so that he may deserve the character of an hard or cruel man; whereas the other having compassion in just the same degree only, yet having resentment or ambition in a lower degree, his compassion may prevail over them so as to influence his actions and to denominate his temper compassionate. So that, how strange soever it may appear to people who do not attend to the thing, yet it is quite manifest that, when we say one man is more resenting or compassionate than another, this does not necessarily imply that one has the principle of resentment or of compassion stronger than the other. For if the proportion which resentment or compassion bears to other inward principles is greater in one than in the other, this is itself sufficient to denominate one more resenting or compassionate than the other.

[11] Further, the whole system, as I may speak, of affections (including rationality), which constitute the heart, as this word is used in Scrip-

ture and on moral subjects, are each and all of them stronger in some than
in others. Now the proportion which the two general affections, benevolence and self-love, bear to each other, according to this interpretation of
the text, denominates men's character as to virtue. Suppose then one man
to have the principle of benevolence in an higher degree than another, it
will not follow from hence that his general temper or character or actions
will be more benevolent than the other's. For he may have self-love in
such a degree as quite to prevail over benevolence, so that it may have no
influence at all upon his actions; whereas benevolence in the other person,
though in a lower degree, may yet be the strongest principle in his heart,
and strong enough to be the guide of his actions so as to demoninate him
a good and virtuous man. The case is here as in scales: it is not one weight,
considered in itself, which determines whether the scale shall ascend or
descend, but this depends upon the proportion which that one weight
hath to the other.

[12] It being thus manifest that the influence which benevolence has
upon our actions, and how far it goes toward forming our character, is
not determined by the degree itself of this principle in our mind, but by
the proportion it has to self-love and other principles, a comparison also
being made in the texts between self-love and the love of our neighbor;
these joint considerations afforded sufficient occasion for treating here
of that proportion; it plainly is implied in the precept, though it should
be questioned whether it be the exact meaning of the words "as thyself."

[13] Love of our neighbor then must bear some proportion to self-love,
and virtue to be sure consists in the due proportion.[7] What this due proportion is, whether as a principle in the mind or as exerted in actions, can
be judged of only from our nature and condition in this world. Of the
degree in which affections and the principles of action, considered in themselves, prevail, we have no measure; let us then proceed to the course of
behavior, the actions they produce.

[14] Both our nature and condition require that each particular man
should make particular provision for himself; and the inquiry what proportion benevolence should have to self-love, when brought down to practice, will be what is a competent care and provision for ourselves. And
how certain soever it be that each man must determine this for himself,
and how ridiculous soever it would be for any to attempt to determine it
for another, yet it is to be observed that the proportion is real, and that a
competent provision has a bound, and that it cannot be all which we can
possibly get and keep within our grasp, without legal injustice. Mankind
almost universally bring in vanity—supplies for what is called a life of
pleasure, covetousness, or imaginary notions of superiority over others—
to determine this question; but every one who desires to act a proper part
in society would do well to consider how far any of them come in to determine it, in the way of moral consideration. All that can be said is, supposing, what, as the world goes, is so much to be supposed that it is scarce to

7. [See Butler's note on Serm. III. 2.]

be mentioned, that persons do not neglect what they really owe to themselves; the more of their care and thought, and of their fortune, they employ in doing good to their follow creatures, the nearer they come up to
the law of perfection, "Thou shalt love thy neighbour as thyself."[8]

[15] Thirdly, if the words "as thyself" were to be understood of an
equality of affection, it would not be attended with those consequences
which perhaps may be thought to follow from it. Suppose a person to have
the same settled regard to others as to himself, that in every deliberate
scheme or pursuit he took their interest into the account in the same degree
as his own, so far as an equality of affection would produce this, yet he
would in fact, and ought to be, much more taken up and employed about
himself and his own concerns than about others and their interests. For,
besides the one common affection toward himself and his neighbor, he
would have several other particular affections, passions, appetites, which
he could not possibly feel in common both for himself and others; now
these sensations themselves very much employ us, and have perhaps as
great influence as self-love. So far indeed as self-love and cool reflection
upon what is for our interest would set us on work to gain a supply of our
own several wants, so far the love of our neighbor would make us do the
same for him; but the degree in which we are put upon seeking and making
use of the means of gratification, by the feeling of those affections, appetites, and passions, must necessarily be peculiar to ourselves.

[16] That there are particular passions (suppose shame, resentment),
which men seem to have and feel in common, both for themselves and
others, makes no alteration in respect to those passions and appetites
which cannot possibly be thus felt in common. From hence (and perhaps
more things of the like kind might be mentioned) it follows that though
there were an equality of affection to both, yet regards to ourselves would
be more prevalent than attention to the concerns of others.

[17] And from moral considerations it ought to be so, supposing still
the equality of affection commanded, because we are in a peculiar manner,
as I may speak, intrusted with ourselves, and therefore care of our own
interests, as well as of our conduct, particularly belongs to us.

[18] To these things must be added that moral obligations can extend
no further than to natural possibilities. Now we have a perception of our
own interests, like consciousness of our own existence, which we always
carry about with us; and which, in its continuation, kind, and degree,
seems impossible to be felt in respect to the interest of others.

[19] From all these things it fully appears that though we were to love
our neighbor in the same degree as we love ourselves, so far as this is
possible, yet the care of ourselves, of the individual, would not be ne-

8. [At the end of § 14, Ed. I. added the words: "A comparison being made in the
text between self-love and the love of our neighbour, and it being evident that the
love of others which includes in it all virtues must necessarily be in due proportion
to the love of ourselves; these joint considerations afforded sufficient occasion for
treating here of that proportion. It is plainly implied in the precept, though it should
not be thought the exact sense of the words *as thyself*."]

glected; the apprehended danger of which seems to be the only objection against understanding the precept in this strict sense.

[20] III. The general temper of mind which the due love of our neighbor would form us to, and the influence it would have upon our behavior in life, is now to be considered.

[21] The temper and behavior of charity is explained at large in that known passage of St. Paul: "Charity suffereth long, and is kind; charity envieth not, doth not behave itself unseemly, seeketh not her own, thinketh no evil, beareth all things, believeth all things, hopeth all things."[9] As to the meaning of the expressions, "seeketh not her own, thinketh no evil, believeth all things," however those expressions may be explained away, this meekness, and in some degree easiness of temper, readiness to forego our right for the sake of peace as well as in the way of compassion, freedom from mistrust, and disposition to believe well of our neighbor— this general temper, I say, accompanies and is plainly the effect of love and goodwill. And though such is the world in which we live, that experience and knowledge of it not only may but must beget in us greater regard to ourselves, and doubtfulness of the characters of others, than is natural to mankind; yet these ought not to be carried further than the nature and course of things make necessary. It is still true, even in the present state of things, bad as it is, that a real good man had rather be deceived than be suspicious, had rather forego his own right than run the venture of doing even a hard thing. This is the general temper of that charity of which the apostle asserts that if he had it not, giving his "body to be burned would avail him nothing"; and which he says "shall never fail."

[22] The happy influence of this temper extends to every different relation and circumstance in human life. It plainly renders a man better, more to be desired, as to all the respects and relations we can stand in to each other. The benevolent man is disposed to make use of all external advantages in such a manner as shall contribute to the good of others as well as to his own satisfaction. His own satisfaction consists in this. He will be easy and kind to his dependents, compassionate to the poor and distressed, friendly to all with whom he has to do. This includes the good neighbor, parent, master, magistrate; and such a behavior would plainly make dependence, inferiority, and even servitude, easy. So that a good or charitable man of superior rank in wisdom, fortune, authority, is a common blessing to the place he lives in—happiness grows under his influence. This good principle in inferiors would discover itself in paying respect, gratitude, obedience, as due. It were therefore, methinks, one just way of trying one's own character to ask ourselves, Am I in reality a better master or servant, a better friend, a better neighbor, than such and such persons whom, perhaps, I may think not to deserve the character of virtue and religion so much as myself?

[23] And as to the spirit of party, which unhappily prevails amongst mankind, whatever are the distinctions which serve for a supply to it, some

9. *I Cor.* XIII: 4-7.

or other of which have obtained in all ages and countries: one who is thus friendly to his kind will immediately make due allowances for it, as what cannot but be amongst such creatures as men, in such a world as this. And as wrath and fury and overbearing upon these occasions proceed, as I may speak, from men's feeling only on their own side, so a common feeling, for others as well as for ourselves, would render us sensible to this truth—which it is strange can have so little influence—that we ourselves differ from others just as much as they do from us. I put the matter in this way, because it can scarce be expected that the generality of men should see that those things which are made the occasions of dissension and fomenting the party spirit are really nothing at all; but it may be expected from all people, how much soever they are in earnest about their respective peculiarities, that humanity and common goodwill to their fellow creatures should moderate and restrain that wretched spirit.

[24] This good temper of charity likewise would prevent strife and enmity arising from other occasions; it would prevent our giving just cause of offense, and our taking it without cause. And in cases of real injury, a good man will make all the allowances which are to be made, and without any attempts of retaliation, he will only consult his own and other men's security for the future, against injustice and wrong.

[25] IV. I proceed to consider, lastly, what is affirmed of the precept now explained, that it comprehends in it all others; that is, that to love our neighbor as ourselves includes in it all virtues.

[26] Now the way in which every maxim of conduct, or general speculative assertion, when it is to be explained at large, should be treated is to show what are the particular truths which were designed to be comprehended under such a general observation, how far it is strictly true; and then the limitations, restrictions, and exceptions, if there be exceptions, with which it is to be understood.[10] But it is only the former of these, namely, how far the assertion in the text holds, and the ground of the preeminence assigned to the precept of it, which in strictness comes into our present consideration.

[27] However, in almost everything that is said, there is somewhat to be understood beyond what is explicitly laid down, and which we of course supply—somewhat, I mean, which would not be commonly called a restriction or limitation. Thus, when benevolence is said to be the sum of virtue, it is not spoken of as a blind propension, but as a principle in reasonable creatures, and so to be directed by their reason; for reason and reflection comes into our notion of a moral agent. And that will lead us to consider distant consequences as well as the immediate tendency of an action; it will teach us that the care of some persons, suppose children and families, is particularly committed to our charge by Nature and Providence, as also that there are other circumstances, suppose friendship or former obligations, which require that we do good to some, preferably to others. Reason, considered merely as subservient to benevolence, as assist-

10. [See, further, on these, § 31 note.]

ing to produce the greatest good, will teach us to have particular regard to these relations and circumstances; because it is plainly for the good of the world that they should be regarded. And as there are numberless cases in which, notwithstanding appearances, we are not competent judges, whether a particular action will upon the whole do good or harm, reason in the same way will teach us to be cautious how we act in these cases of uncertainty. It will suggest to our consideration which is the safer side, how liable we are to be led wrong by passion and private interest, and what regard is due to laws and the judgment of mankind. All these things must come into consideration were it only in order to determine which way of acting is likely to produce the greatest good. Thus, upon supposition that it were in the strictest sense true, without limitation, that benevolence includes in it all virtues, yet reason must come in as its guide and director in order to attain its own end, the end of benevolence, the greatest public good. Reason then being thus included, let us now consider the truth of the assertion itself.

[28] First, it is manifest that nothing can be of consequence to mankind or any creature, but happiness. This then is all which any person can, in strictness of speaking, be said to have a right to. We can therefore "owe no man anything,"[11] but only further and promote his happiness, according to our abilities. And therefore a disposition and endeavor to do good to all with whom we have to do, in the degree and manner which the different relations we stand in to them require, is a discharge of all the obligations we are under to them.

[29] As human nature is not one simple uniform thing, but a composition of various parts, body, spirit, appetites, particular passions, and affections, for each of which reasonable self-love would lead men to have due regard and make suitable provision, so society consists of various parts to which we stand in different respects and relations; and just benevolence would as surely lead us to have due regard to each of these, and behave as the respective relations require. [Reasonable][12] goodwill and right behavior toward our fellow creatures are in a manner the same, only that the former expresseth the principle as it is in the mind, the latter, the principle as it were become external, that is, exerted in actions.

[30] And so far as temperance, sobriety, and moderation in sensual pleasures, and the contrary vices, have any respect to our fellow creatures, any influence upon their quiet, welfare, and happiness, as they always have a real and often a near influence upon it, so far it is manifest those virtues may be produced by the love of our neighbor, and that the contrary vices would be prevented by it. Indeed, if men's regard to themselves will not restrain them from excess, it may be thought little probable that their love to others will be sufficient; but the reason is that their love to others is not, any more than their regard to themselves, just and in its due degree.

11. [*Rom.* XIII: 8: "Owe no man anything, but to love one another."]

12. [Not in Ed. I.]

There are however manifest instances of persons kept sober and temperate from regard to their affairs and the welfare of those who depend upon them. And it is obvious to everyone that habitual excess, a dissolute course of life, implies a general neglect of the duties we owe toward our friends, our families, and our country.

[31] From hence it is manifest that the common virtues and the common vices of mankind may be traced up to benevolence, or the want of it. And this entitles the precept, "Thou shalt love thy neighbour as thyself," to the preeminence given to it; and is a justification of the Apostle's assertion that all other commandments are comprehended in it, whatever cautions and restrictions[13] there are, which might require to be considered if we were to state particularly and at length what is virtue and right behavior in mankind. But,

[32] Secondly, it might be added that in a higher and more general way of consideration, leaving out the particular nature of creatures and the particular circumstances in which they are placed, benevolence seems in the strictest sense to include in it all that is good and worthy; all that is good, which we have any distinct particular notion of. We have no clear conception of any positive moral attribute in the Supreme Being but what may be resolved up into goodness. And if we consider a reasonable creature or moral agent, without regard to the particular relations and circumstances in which he is placed, we cannot conceive anything else to come in toward determining whether he is to be ranked in an higher or

---

13. For instance: as we are not competent judges what is upon the whole for the good of the world, there may be other immediate ends appointed us to pursue, besides that one of doing good or producing happiness. Though the good of the creation be the only end of the Author of it, yet He may have laid us under particular obligations, which we may discern and feel ourselves under, quite distinct from a perception that the observance or violation of them is for the happiness or misery of our fellow creatures. And this is in fact the case. For there are certain dispositions of mind, and certain actions, which are in themselves approved or disapproved by mankind, abstracted from the consideration of their tendency to the happiness or misery of the world; approved or disapproved by reflection, by that principle within, which is the guide of life, the judge of right and wrong. Numberless instances of this kind might be mentioned. There are pieces of treachery which in themselves appear base and detestable to every one. There are actions which perhaps can scarce have any other general name given them than indecencies, which yet are odious and shocking to human nature. There is such a thing as meanness, a little mind; which, as it is quite distinct from incapacity, so it raises a dislike and disapprobation quite different from that contempt which men are too apt to have of mere folly. On the other hand, what we call greatness of mind is the object of another sort of approbation than superior understanding. Fidelity, honor, strict justice are themselves approved in the highest degree, abstracted from the consideration of their tendency. Now, whether it be thought that each of these are connected with benevolence in our nature, and so may be considered as the same thing with it, or whether some of them be thought an inferior kind of virtues and vices, somewhat like natural beauties and deformities, or lastly, plain exceptions to the general rule—thus much however is certain that the things now instanced in, and numberless others, are approved or disapproved by mankind in general, in quite another view than as conducive to the happiness or misery of the world.

lower class of virtuous beings, but the higher or lower degree in which that principle, and what is manifestly connected with it, prevail in him.

[33] That which we more strictly call piety, or the love of God, and which is an essential part of a right temper, some may perhaps imagine no way connected with benevolence; yet surely they must be connected if there be indeed in being an object infinitely good. Human nature is so constituted that every good affection implies the love of itself, that is, becomes the object of a new affection in the same person. Thus to be righteous implies in it the love of righteousness; to be benevolent, the love of benevolence; to be good, the love of goodness, whether this righteousness, benevolence, or goodness be viewed as in our own mind or in another's; and the love of God as being perfectly good is the love of perfect goodness contemplated in a being or person. Thus morality and religion, virtue and piety, will at last necessarily coincide, run up into one and the same point, and love will be in all senses "the end of the commandment."[14]

O Almighty God, inspire us with this divine principle; kill in us all the seeds of envy and ill will; and help us, by cultivating within ourselves the love of our neighbor, to improve in the love of Thee. Thou hast placed us in various kindreds, friendships, and relations, as the school of discipline for our affections; help us, by the due exercise of them, to improve to perfection, till all partial affection be lost in that entire universal one, and Thou, O God, shalt be all in all.

14. [*I Tim.* I: 5.]

A DISSERTATION
UPON THE NATURE OF VIRTUE[1]

[1] THAT which renders beings capable of moral government is their having a moral nature and moral faculties of perception and of action. Brute creatures are impressed and actuated by various instincts and propensions; so also are we. But additional to this, we have a capacity of reflecting upon actions and characters, and making them an object to our thought; and in doing this, we naturally and unavoidably approve some actions, under the peculiar view of their being virtuous and of good desert, and disapprove others as vicious and of ill desert. That we have this moral approving and disapproving[2] faculty is certain from our experiencing it in ourselves, and recognizing it in each other. It appears from our exercising it unavoidably, in the approbation and disapprobation even of feigned characters; from the words "right" and "wrong," "odious" and "amiable," "base" and "worthy," with many others of like signification in all languages applied to actions and characters; from the many written systems of morals which suppose it, since it cannot be imagined that all these authors, throughout all these treatises, had absolutely no meaning at all to their words, or a meaning merely chimerical; from our natural sense of gratitude, which implies a distinction between merely being the instrument of good and intending it; from the like distinction every one makes between injury and mere harm, which Hobbes says is peculiar to mankind, and between injury and just punishment, a distinction plainly natural, prior to the consideration of human laws. It is manifest great part of common language, and of common behavior over the world, is formed upon supposition of such a moral faculty, whether called conscience, moral reason, moral sense, or divine reason; whether considered as a sentiment of the understanding or as a perception of the heart, or, which seems the truth, as including both. Nor is it at all doubtful in the general what course of action this faculty, or practical discerning power within us, approves and what it disapproves. For, as much as it has been disputed wherein virtue

---

1. [This Dissertation belongs to the *Analogy*, where it forms an appendix to I. ch. 3, "Of the Moral Government of God."]

2. This way of speaking is taken from Epictetus,[3] and is made use of as seeming the most full, and least liable to cavil. And the moral faculty may be understood to have these two epithets δοκιμαστικὴ and ἀποδοκιμαστικὴ, upon a double account; because, upon a survey of actions, whether before or after they are done, it determines them to be good or evil; and also because it determines itself to be the guide of action and of life, in contradistinction from all other faculties, or natural principles of action, in the very same manner as speculative reason *directly* and naturally judges of speculative truth and falsehood; and at the same time is attended with a consciousness upon *reflection* that the natural right to judge of them belongs to it.

3. Arr. Epict. lib. i. cap. I.

consists, or whatever ground for doubt there may be about particulars, yet, in general, there is in reality an universally acknowledged standard of it. It is that which all ages and all countries have made profession of in public; it is that which every man you meet puts on the show of; it is that which the primary and fundamental laws of all civil constitutions over the face of the earth make it their business and endeavor to enforce the practice of upon mankind, namely, justice, veracity and regard to common good. It being manifest then, in general, that we have such a faculty or discernment as this, it may be of use to remark some things more distinctly concerning it.

[2] *First,* it ought to be observed that the object of this faculty is actions,[4] comprehending under that name active or practical principles— those principles from which men would act if occasions and circumstances gave them power; and which, when fixed and habitual in any person, we call his character. It does not appear that brutes have the least reflex sense of actions, as distinguished from events, or that will and design, which constitute the very nature of actions as such, are at all an object to their perception. But to ours they are; and they are the object, and the only one, of the approving and disapproving faculty. Acting, conduct, behavior, abstracted from all regard to what is in fact and event the consequence of it, is itself the natural object of the moral discernment, as speculative truth and falsehood is of speculative reason. Intention of such and such consequences, indeed, is always included, for it is part of the action itself; but though the intended good or bad consequences do not follow, we have exactly the same sense of the action as if they did. In like manner we think well or ill of characters, abstracted from all consideration of the good or the evil, which persons of such characters have it actually in their power to do. We never, in the moral way, applaud or blame either ourselves or others for what we enjoy or what we suffer, or for having impressions made upon us, which we consider as altogether out of our power, but only for what we do or would have done had it been in our power; or for what we leave undone, which we might have done or would have left undone, though we could have done it.

[3] *Secondly,* our sense or discernment of actions as morally good or evil implies in it a sense or discernment of them as of good or ill desert. It may be difficult to explain this perception so as to answer all the questions which may be asked concerning it; but everyone speaks of such and such actions as deserving punishment; and it is not, I suppose, pretended that they have absolutely no meaning at all to the expression. Now the meaning plainly is not that we conceive it for the good of society that the doer of such actions should be made to suffer. For if, unhappily, it were resolved that a man who, by some innocent action, was infected with the plague should be left to perish lest, by other people's coming near him, the infection should spread, no one would say he deserved this treatment.

---

4. "Οὐδὲ ἡ ἀρετὴ καὶ κακία — ἐν πείσει, ἀλλὰ ενεργεία," M. Anton, lib. ix. 16; *"Virtutis laus omnis in actione consistit,"* Cic., *Off.,* lib. i. cap. 6.

Innocence and ill desert are inconsistent ideas. Ill desert always supposes guilt; and if one be no part of the other, yet they are evidently and naturally connected in our mind. The sight of a man in misery raises our compassion toward him, and, if this misery be inflicted on him by another, our indignation against the author of it. But when we are informed that the sufferer is a villain and is punished only for his treachery or cruelty, our compassion exceedingly lessens, and in many instances our indignation wholly subsides. Now what produces this effect is the conception of that in the sufferer which we call ill desert. Upon considering then, or viewing together, our notion of vice and that of misery, there results a third—that of ill desert. And thus there is in human creatures an association of the two ideas, natural and moral evil, wickedness and punishment. If this association were merely artificial or accidental, it were nothing; but being most unquestionably natural, it greatly concerns us to attend to it, instead of endeavoring to explain it away.

[4] It may be observed further, concerning our perception of good and of ill desert, that the former is very weak with respect to common instances of virtue. One reason of which may be that it does not appear to a spectator, how far such instances of virtue proceed from a virtuous principle, or in what degree this principle is prevalent; since a very weak regard to virtue may be sufficient to make men act well in many common instances. And on the other hand, our perception of ill desert in vicious actions lessens, in proportion to the temptations men are thought to have had to such vices. For vice in human creatures consisting chiefly in the absence or want of the virtuous principle, though a man be overcome, suppose, by tortures, it does not from thence appear to what degree the virtuous principle was wanting. All that appears is that he had it not in such a degree as to prevail over the temptation; but possibly he had it in a degree which would have rendered him proof against common temptations.

[5] *Thirdly,* our perception of vice and ill desert arises from, and is the result of, a comparison of actions with the nature and capacities of the agent. For the mere neglect of doing what we ought to do would, in many cases, be determined by all men to be in the highest degree vicious. And his determination must arise from such comparison, and be the result of it; because such neglect would not be vicious in creatures of other natures and capacities, as brutes. And it is the same also with respect to positive vices, or such as consist in doing what we ought not. For every one has a different sense of harm done by an idiot, madman, or child, and by one of mature and common understanding, though the action of both, including the intention, which is part of the action, be the same; as it may be, since idiots and madmen, as well as children, are capable not only of doing mischief, but also of intending it. Now this difference must arise from somewhat discerned in the nature or capacities of one, which renders the action vicious; and the want of which, in the other, renders the same action innocent or less vicious; and this plainly supposes a comparison, whether reflected upon or not, between the action and capacities of the agent, previous to our determining an action to be vicious. And hence

arises a proper application of the epithets "incongruous," "unsuitable," "disproportionate," "unfit" to actions which our moral faculty determines to be vicious.

[6] *Fourthly,* it deserves to be considered whether men are more at liberty, in point of morals, to make themselves miserable without reason than to make other people so, or dissolutely to neglect their own greater good, for the sake of a present lesser gratification, than they are to neglect the good of others whom nature has committed to their care. It should seem that a due concern about our own interest or happiness, and a reasonable endeavor to secure and promote it, which is, I think, very much the meaning of the word "prudence" in our language—it should seem that this is virtue, and the contrary behavior faulty and blamable, since, in the calmest way of reflection, we approve of the first, and condemn the other conduct, both in ourselves and others. This approbation and disapprobation are altogether different from mere desire of our own or of their happiness, and from sorrow upon missing it. For the object or occasion of this last kind of perception is satisfaction or uneasiness, whereas the object of the first is active behavior. In one case, what our thoughts fix upon is our condition, in the other, our conduct. It is true, indeed, that nature has not given us so sensible a disapprobation of imprudence and folly, either in *ourselves* or *others,* as of falsehood, injustice and cruelty; I suppose, because that constant habitual sense of private interest and good, which we always carry about with us, renders such sensible disapprobation less necessary, less wanting, to keep us from imprudently neglecting our own happiness and foolishly injuring ourselves, than it is necessary and wanting to keep us from injuring others to whose good we cannot have so strong and constant a regard; and also because imprudence and folly appearing to bring its own punishment more immediately and constantly than injurious behavior, it less needs the additional punishment which would be inflicted upon it by others had they the same sensible indignation against it as against injustice and fraud and cruelty. Besides, unhappiness being in itself the natural object of compassion, the unhappiness which people bring upon themselves, though it be willfully, excites in us some pity for them; and this, of course, lessens our displeasure against them. But still it is matter of experience that we are formed so as to reflect very severely upon the greater instances of imprudent neglect and foolish rashness, both in ourselves and others. In instances of this kind, men often say of themselves with remorse, and of others with some indignation, that they deserved to suffer such calamities because they brought them upon themselves and would not take warning. Particularly when persons come to poverty and distress by a long course of extravagance and after frequent admonitions, though without falsehood or injustice; we plainly do not regard such people as alike objects of compassion with those who are brought into the same condition by unavoidable accidents. From these things it appears that prudence is a species of virtue, and folly of vice, meaning by "folly" somewhat quite different from mere incapacity—a thoughtless want of that regard and attention to our own hap-

piness which we had capacity for. And this the word properly includes, and, as it seems, in its usual acceptation, for we scarcely apply it to brute creatures.

[7] However, if any person be disposed to dispute the matter, I shall very willingly give him up the words "virtue" and "vice," as not applicable to prudence and folly, but must beg leave to insist that the faculty within us, which is the judge of actions, approves of prudent actions, and disapproves imprudent ones; I say prudent and imprudent *actions* as such, and considered distinctly from the happiness or misery which they occasion. And, by the way, this observation may help to determine what justness there is in that objection against religion, that it teaches us to be interested and selfish.

[8] *Fifthly,* without inquiring how far, and in what sense, virtue is resolvable into benevolence, and vice into the want of it, it may be proper to observe that benevolence and the want of it, singly considered, are in no sort the whole of virtue and vice. For if this were the case, in the review of one's own character, or that of others, our moral understanding and moral sense would be indifferent to everything but the degrees in which benevolence prevailed, and the degrees in which it was wanting. That is, we should neither approve of benevolence to some persons rather than to others, nor disapprove injustice and falsehood upon any other account than merely as an overbalance of happiness was foreseen likely to be produced by the first, and of misery by the second. But now, on the contrary, suppose two men competitors for anything whatever, which would be of equal advantage to each of them; though nothing indeed would be more impertinent than for a stranger to busy himself to get one of them preferred to the other, yet such endeavor would be virtue, in behalf of a friend or benefactor, abstracted from all consideration of distant consequences, as that examples of gratitude, and the cultivation of friendship, would be of general good to the world. Again, suppose one man should, by fraud or violence, take from another the fruit of his labor, with intent to give it to a third who he thought would have as much pleasure from it as would balance the pleasure which the first possessor would have had in the enjoyment, and his vexation in the loss of it; suppose also that no bad consequences would follow, yet such an action would surely be vicious. Nay further, were treachery, violence and injustice not otherwise vicious than as foreseen likely to produce an overbalance of misery to society, then, if in any case a man could procure to himself as great advantage by an act of injustice as the whole foreseen inconvenience, likely to be brought upon others by it, would amount to, such a piece of injustice would not be faulty or vicious at all; because it would be no more than, in any other case, for a man to prefer his own satisfaction to another's in equal degrees. The fact then appears to be that we are constituted so as to condemn falsehood, unprovoked violence, injustice, and to approve of benevolence to some, preferably to others, abstracted from all consideration which conduct is likeliest to produce an overbalance of happiness or misery. And therefore, were the Author of

Nature to propose nothing to himself as an end but the production of happiness, were his moral character merely that of benevolence, yet ours is not so. Upon that supposition, indeed, the only reason of his giving us the above-mentioned approbation of benevolence to some persons rather than others, and disapprobation of falsehood, unprovoked violence, and injustice, must be that he foresaw this constitution of our nature would produce more happiness than forming us with a temper of mere general benevolence. But still, since this is our constitution, falsehood, violence, injustice must be vice in us, and benevolence to some, preferably to others, virtue, abstracted from all consideration of the overbalance of evil or good, which they may appear likely to produce.

[9] Now if human creatures are endued with such a moral nature as we have been explaining, or with a moral faculty the natural object of which is actions, moral government must consist in rendering them happy and unhappy, in rewarding and punishing them as they follow, neglect or depart from, the moral rule of action interwoven in their nature, or suggested and enforced by this moral faculty[5]—in rewarding and punishing them upon account of their so doing.

[10] I am not sensible that I have, in this fifth observation, contradicted what any author designed to assert. But some of great and distinguished merit have, I think, expressed themselves in a manner which may occasion some danger to careless readers, of imagining the whole of virtue to consist in singly aiming, according to the best of their judgment, at promoting the happiness of mankind in the present state; and the whole of vice in doing what they foresee, or might foresee, is likely to produce an overbalance of unhappiness in it; than which mistakes, none can be conceived more terrible.[6] For it is certain that some of the most shocking instances of injustice, adultery, murder, perjury, and even of persecution, may, in many supposable cases, not have the appearance of being likely to produce an overbalance of misery in the present state; perhaps sometimes may have the contrary appearance. For this reflection might easily be carried on, but I forbear. The happiness of the world is the concern of him who is the Lord and the Proprietor of it; nor do we know what we are about when we endeavor to promote the good of mankind in any ways but those which he has directed—that is indeed in all ways not contrary to veracity and justice. I speak thus upon supposition of persons really endeavoring, in some sort, to do good without regard to these. But the truth seems to be that such supposed endeavors proceed, almost always, from ambition, the spirit of the party, or some indirect principle, concealed perhaps in great measure from persons themselves. And though it is our business and our duty to endeavor, within the bounds of veracity and justice, to contribute to the ease, convenience, and even cheerfulness and diversion of our fellow creatures, yet, from our short

5. *Analogy,* Pt. I. ch. 6.

6. [The writers referred to are probably Shaftesbury and Hutcheson.]

views, it is greatly uncertain whether this endeavor will in particular instances produce an overbalance of happiness upon the whole, since so many and distant things must come into the account. And that which makes it our duty is that there is some appearance that it will, and no positive appearance sufficient to balance this, on the contrary side; and also, that such benevolent endeavor is a cultivation of that most excellent of all virtuous principles, the active principle of benevolence.

[11] However, though veracity as well as justice is to be our rule of life, it must be added, otherwise a snare will be laid in the way of some plain men, that the use of common forms of speech, generally understood, cannot be falsehood; and in general, that there can be no designed falsehood without designing to deceive. It must likewise be observed that, in numberless cases, a man may be under the strictest obligations to what he foresees will deceive, without his intending it. For it is impossible not to foresee that the words and actions of men, in different ranks and employments, and of different educations, will perpetually be mistaken by each other; and it cannot but be so whilst they will judge with the utmost carelessness, as they daily do, of what they are not, perhaps, enough informed to be competent judges of, even though they considered it with great attention.